Vintage Kitchen Journal

Vintage Kitchen Journal

The perfect place to store your favourite recipes, treasured ideas, hints and tips

This edition published by Parragon Books Ltd in 2013
LOVE FOOD is an imprint of Parragon Books Ltd

Parragon Books Ltd
Chartist House
15–17 Trim Street
Bath BA1 1HA, UK
www.parragon.com/lovefood

ISBN: 978-1-4723-2421-4

Printed in China

Edited by Fiona Biggs
Additional photography and styling by Mike Cooper
Additional home economy by Lincoln Jefferson
Internal design by Sarah Knight

Notes for the Reader
This book uses both metric and imperial measurements. Follow the same units of measurement throughout; do not mix metric and imperial. All spoon measurements are level: teaspoons are assumed to be 5 ml, and tablespoons are assumed to be 15 ml. Unless otherwise stated, milk is assumed to be full fat, eggs and individual vegetables are medium, and pepper is freshly ground black pepper. Unless otherwise stated, all root vegetables should be washed in plain water and peeled prior to using.

For best results, use a food thermometer when cooking meat and poultry – check the latest government guidelines for current advice.

Garnishes, decorations and serving suggestions are all optional and not necessarily included in the recipe ingredients or method.

The times given are an approximate guide only. Preparation times differ according to the techniques used by different people and the cooking times may also vary from those given. Optional ingredients, variations or serving suggestions have not been included in the time calculations.

Recipes using raw or very lightly cooked eggs should be avoided by infants, the elderly, pregnant women, convalescents and anyone suffering from an illness. Pregnant and breastfeeding women are advised to avoid eating peanuts and peanut products. Sufferers from nut allergies should be aware that some of the ready-made ingredients used in the recipes in this book may contain nuts. Always check the packaging before use.

Vegetarians should be aware that some of the ready-made ingredients used in the recipes in this book may contain animal products. Always check the packaging before use.

Picture acknowledgements
Vintage labels © AKaiser/Shutterstock
Close-up notepaper on cork board © Picsfive/Shutterstock
A coffee cup stain © Tyler Olson/Shutterstock
Marking Tape © Samantha Grandy/Shutterstock
Vintage prints and crockery supplied courtesy of iStock Images

Contents

INTRODUCTION

Busy kitchens mean busy cooks, and busy cooks don't always have the time to organise their recipe collection in the way they would like. Magazines, recipe printouts and scribbled ideas can quickly build up and become unusable as you struggle to locate that recipe you found months ago that you are now desperate to make! Enter *Vintage Kitchen Journal*, the essential addition to your cookbook collection!

Vintage Kitchen Journal is an easy way to gather together and safely keep recipes torn from magazines, printed from the internet or handwritten with love and passed down through the generations (with splashes and food stains galore). Invaluable pockets are included for storing cherished recipes, and the useful note section lets you quickly jot down and safely keep any food-related tip if the need arises. There is plenty of space for writing in new recipe ideas from friends and family, creating the ultimate kitchen resource that would rival any store-bought cookbook.

Also included is a selection of classic recipes, savoury and sweet, that will satisfy any food lover. From family dinners to delicious baked treats, there are recipes for every occasion to impress friends and family. With an extensive introduction that covers all the basic cooking techniques and ingredients, *Vintage Kitchen Journal* is all you need to whip up and dish out the most delicious dishes!

A good store of non-perishable foodstuffs is an essential part of any kitchen. Well-stocked cupboards, and perhaps a larder, will ensure you always have a good selection of staple items on hand for any occasion. Regularly check and discard any stored items that are out of date.

OILS

There are many different varieties of oil available these days, but it is not necessary to buy them all. You simply need oil that is suitable for drizzling and for cooking at high temperatures.

OLIVE OIL

This mildly fruity oil is ideal for drizzling over salads. It can range from a champagne colour to bright green. The best oils are cold-pressed – this is a chemical-free process that uses only pressure and produces a low level of acidity. You can also flavour it with different ingredients. For example, try adding some herbs, such as basil leaves, or some garlic to it – after a day or two the oil will become infused with their flavour. Its smoke point (the temperature at which it begins to smoke) is 210°C/410°F.

EXTRA VIRGIN OLIVE OIL

Produced from the first cold-pressing of the olives, this oil has a very low acid level. It is the most expensive type of olive oil and has a peppery, fruity flavour. You can use it for drizzling over salads and hot dishes such as pizzas. Its smoke point is 210°C/410°F.

CORN OIL

This is a good choice for cooking. It has a strong, distinctive flavour that makes it unsuitable for dressings and drizzling. Its smoke point is 210°C/410°F.

SUNFLOWER OIL

This is a good multi-purpose oil that can be used for most cooking purposes. Sunflower oil has a very light flavour and is therefore ideal in dressings. However, it is not recommended for deep-frying because this method needs an oil with a higher smoke point. The smoke point of sunflower oil is 199°C/390°F.

SESAME OIL

This oil is excellent for frying and stir-frying and comes in two varieties: one has a light colour and nutty flavour; the other is darker and has a stronger flavour. Its smoke point is 210°C/410°F.

VEGETABLE OIL

A blend of various oils, mainly rapeseed, soya, coconut and palm. It is best used for frying rather than in salads because it is quite greasy.

SOYA OIL

This economical oil is extracted from soya beans and has a light yellow colour. Like rapeseed oil, its popularity is growing because it is low in saturated fat. It has a strong taste and is unsuitable for dressings or drizzling. Its smoke point is 232°C/450°F, which makes it ideal for all types of cooking, including deep-frying.

VINEGARS

Vinegar adds a lovely, pungent kick to dressings, marinades, sauces and a wide range of dishes. It is available in different varieties, and here are some of the most popular types.

MALT VINEGAR

This is made from malted barley and is available in two varieties: a colourless form, which is very strong and is used for pickling, and a dark brown variety, which is used in chutneys and on traditional British fish and chips. This vinegar is not suitable for dressings.

CIDER VINEGAR

This vinegar is made from apples and has a strong, sharp taste. It is best used with meats and in pickles and chutneys.

WINE VINEGARS

These are available in different varieties, mainly red, white and sherry. They can be used in dressings, marinades and sauces, and can be sprinkled over food.

BALSAMIC VINEGAR

This delicious vinegar is thick, dark and slightly sweet. It is made from grape juice that is aged in barrels over a period of years.

RAPESEED OIL

This oil is gaining in popularity because it is lower in saturated fat than other oils. It also contains the omega-3 essential fatty acid, which is now widely believed to help reduce cholesterol levels. It has a mild flavour making it suitable for salads.

GROUNDNUT OIL

A combination of a very mild flavour and a high smoke point of 232°C/450°F makes groundnut oil extremely versatile. It is suitable for drizzling, dressings and mayonnaise, as well as all forms of cooking, including deep-frying.

PASTA, NOODLES & GRAINS

All these different dried pasta shapes, noodles and grains keep well in the storecupboard. They are ideal for cooking quick, satisfying meals at short notice.

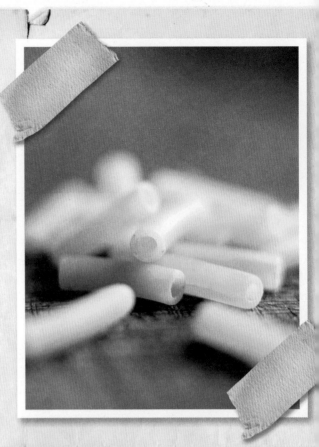

LONG-SHAPED PASTA

There are different varieties of dried long-shaped pastas, including spaghetti, fettuccine (narrow ribbons), tagliatelle (slightly wider ribbons) and vermicelli (very fine, hair-like lengths). These pastas are usually made with durum wheat or wholemeal flour, and may be coloured using ingredients such as spinach (green), beetroot juice (red), tomatoes (orange-red) or even squid ink (black).

SHORT-SHAPED PASTA

Dried short shapes of pasta include conchiglie (shells), fusilli (spirals), farfalle (bows) and tubular varieties such as penne and macaroni. These shapes are particularly good for holding chunky sauces.

OTHER SHAPES OF DRIED PASTA

Other favourite shapes to keep in your storecupboard include lasagne (rectangular sheets) and cannelloni (large tubes).

DRIED NOODLES

Most noodles are associated with Asian cooking. The main difference between noodles and long-shaped pasta is that noodles usually have egg added, such as Chinese egg noodles. Alternatively, sometimes they are made from rice flour. Noodles are very popular in stir-fries and soups. Many varieties need no cooking – you simply soak them in hot water for a few minutes before adding them to the dish of your choice.

LONG-GRAIN RICE

You can buy white and brown varieties of long-grain rice. When cooked, the grains stay dry and separate and do not clump together. This rice is used in savoury dishes.

MEDIUM-GRAIN RICE

These grains are a little shorter than long-grain rice, and more moist. They tend to clump together when cooked. This rice is used in savoury dishes such as Spanish paella and Japanese sushi.

SHORT-GRAIN RICE

This rice has short grains that are more starchy and moist than medium- and long-grain rice. There are different varieties, including pearl rice (used in Asian cooking) and arborio and carnaroli rice (used in risottos).

EASY-COOK RICE

The grains in easy-cook rice are polished and partly boiled so that they are quick and easy to cook and stay fluffy and separate. Easy-cook rice is a convenient alternative to white or brown rice, but does not have as much flavour.

WILD RICE

This is a marsh grass that is cultivated in the United States of America and Canada. The grains are long and black and have a nutty flavour. Wild rice is expensive, so for economy reasons it is often mixed with less expensive brown long-grain rice.

BULGAR WHEAT

This comprises wheat kernels that have had the bran removed. They are then steamed, dried and ground into different degrees of coarseness. The result is a golden-brown grain that has a nutty flavour. It can be cooked like rice and is also excellent in salads.

COUSCOUS

This is not a true grain, but pieces of semolina dough that have been rolled, dampened and coated with a fine wheat flour. It makes a fine accompaniment to savoury dishes.

POLENTA

This yellow grain is made from cornmeal.

PULSES

All pulses except lentils and split peas need soaking for at least 8 hours, then boiling rapidly for 10 minutes before cooking for around 45 minutes.

CANNELLINI BEANS

A type of haricot bean, these long, creamy white beans are excellent in soups and salads.

RED KIDNEY BEANS

These red, kidney-shaped beans can be added to soups, salads, stews and other savoury dishes such as chilli con carne. They can cause food poisoning if not boiled rapidly for at least 10 minutes.

ADUKI BEANS

These small red beans are popular in Japanese cooking, especially coated with sugar. They are also good in soups and salads.

BUTTER BEANS

These white, kidney-shaped beans are excellent in soups and salads.

SOYA BEANS

Although most soya beans are yellow, they can also be black, brown or green. They are much richer in nutrients than the other pulses, and are particularly full of protein, as well as iron and calcium. Soya beans are used to make cooking oils and margarine, flour, soya milk and cheeses, soy sauce, tofu, miso and textured vegetable protein.

CHICKPEAS

These round, beige pulses have a nutty flavour and are excellent in soups, stews and salads, as well as ground up in dips such as hummus. They need a longer soaking and cooking time than many pulses, so it is good to keep some canned chickpeas on hand for when you are short of time.

LENTILS

These tiny, disc-shaped pulses are available in different varieties and colours. Red and orange lentils become mushy when cooked and are therefore ideal puréed and used in soups and sauces. The green and continental brown varieties (Puy lentils) keep their shape when cooked and are ideal in warm winter salads, sauces, stews and other savoury dishes.

SPLIT PEAS

These small peas are disc-shaped and split along a natural seam. They can be yellow or green and are excellent cooked and puréed. They are also good in soups, bakes and other savoury dishes.

BLACK-EYED BEANS

These small beige beans have a circular black 'eye'. They are commonly found in Chinese cooking and are very popular in sauces, stir-fries and soups.

BORLOTTI BEANS

These oval-shaped beans have pale pink to maroon streaked skin. They are creamy when cooked and are excellent in soups, dips and other savoury dishes.

NUTS & SEEDS

Nuts and seeds can quickly go rancid because of their high oil content. Store nuts with shells in a cool, dry place. If shelled, refrigerate in airtight containers.

ALMONDS

These lozenge-shaped nuts have a thin brown covering and a cream centre. They come in two types, sweet and bitter, but it is the sweet variety that is normally used. Available whole, blanched, chopped and crystallized, they are excellent in both savoury and sweet dishes.

HAZELNUTS

These small, round nuts have a brown covering and a cream interior, and a rich, sweet flavour. They are especially popular in muesli and cereals, savoury dishes and bakes, such as nut loaf, and in sweet dishes including cakes and biscuits.

WALNUTS

These nuts have a large, round, wrinkled shell and two double lobes inside. The nuts have a delicious creamy taste and are good in salads and savoury bakes, as well as sweet dishes and cakes. They also make a very flavourful oil.

PECAN NUTS

These nuts are golden brown with a beige interior. They have a very high fat content and are used in a variety of savoury dishes and desserts.

CASHEW NUTS

These creamy, butter-flavoured, kidney-shaped nuts have a high fat content and are delicious roasted and added to stir-fries and bakes.

PISTACHIO NUTS

These pale green nuts have a delicate flavour. They are often used in stuffings and also to decorate desserts.

PINE KERNELS

These small, oval nuts are excellent toasted or dry-fried.

SAUCES, PASTES & CONDIMENTS

A good selection of sauces and condiments is invaluable in the kitchen, and will ensure you always have the right ingredients on hand to add exciting and interesting flavours to your dishes.

TOMATO KETCHUP

This sauce is popular in British cooking and is eaten with cooked foods such as chips and burgers. It is also good as an ingredient in dressings and relishes.

BROWN SAUCE

This strongly flavoured sauce is traditionally served with a fried breakfast.

SOY SAUCE

This sauce is essential for stir-fries and other Asian dishes. The Chinese version is salty, and the Japanese version is sweeter.

HOISIN SAUCE

This sweet, soya-based sauce with a sticky texture is very popular in Chinese cooking. It is known by various names including Peking sauce.

WORCESTERSHIRE SAUCE

This strongly flavoured sauce is made with onions, molasses and anchovies, and is used to season meats, gravies and soups.

PESTO SAUCE

Made from basil, garlic, pine kernels, Parmesan cheese and olive oil, pesto is good with pasta.

TABASCO SAUCE

This very hot chilli sauce is used in dishes such as Mexican salsa to give them a kick. It is also used to season certain cocktails.

THAI FISH SAUCE (NAM PLA

This salty sauce is made from fermented fish and has a very strong taste and smell. It is used to flavour Thai dishes and as a table condiment.

OTHER ITEMS

Here is a selection of other items you will find useful to keep in your storecupboard.

STOCK CUBES

These are very convenient for soups, casseroles and other dishes, particularly if you do not have enough time to make fresh stock.

MISO

This is a paste made from fermented soya beans. It is used in Japanese cooking to thicken and flavour soups and other dishes.

TOMATO PURÉE

This is a tomato paste that is useful in sauces and soups because of its intense flavour.

CANNED TOMATOES

These can be used in a wide variety of dishes, from sauces and soups to stews and casseroles.

SUN-DRIED TOMATOES

These are very good in Italian recipes, particularly salads, pastas and bread.

CANNED PULSES

You can buy a wide variety of canned beans, such as red kidney beans and chickpeas, which will save you time because you do not have to soak them or cook them. Tins of baked beans in tomato sauce are also indispensable for quick meals.

CANNED FISH

Canned fish, such as tuna, salmon, crab, anchovies, sardines and pilchards, are versatile items to have in the storecupboard. They are particularly useful when added to pasta.

OLIVES

It is always useful to keep a tin or bottle of olives on hand. They make ideal tapas for unexpected guests and are delicious in salads and pastas and on pizzas.

MUSTARDS

You can buy different types of mustard. Dijon mustard has a strong flavour and is used in dips and dressings. English mustard is very hot and useful in dips and dressings. Coarse-grain mustard is usually milder, and is good with a variety of savoury dishes, especially meats.

PICKLED FOODS

Onions, gherkins and capers make perfect accompaniments and garnishes for meat and vegetable dishes.

CHOCOLATE & COCOA POWDER

These are useful for desserts and baked goods, and also for some savoury dishes.

VANILLA

You can buy vanilla in pod or liquid form (extract) to use as a flavouring. It is particularly delicious in desserts.

Seasonal Food Chart

	SPRING			SUMMER			AUTUMN			WINTER		
	EARLY	MID	LATE	EARLY	MID	LATE	EARLY	MID	LATE	EARLY	MID	LATE
FISH & SEAFOOD												
Clams	●	●					●	●	●	●	●	●
Cod	●	●	●	●	●	●	●	●	●	●	●	●
Haddock			●	●	●	●	●	●	●	●	●	●
Lobster		●	●	●	●	●	●	●	●	●		
Mackerel			●	●	●	●	●	●			●	●
Mussels	●						●	●	●	●	●	●
Place			●				●	●	●	●	●	●
Prawns*	●	●	●	●	●		●	●	●	●	●	●
Salmon			●	●	●	●	●	●				
Sardines			●	●	●	●	●	●	●			
Scallops	●							●	●	●	●	●
Sea bass	●						●	●	●	●	●	●
Shrimp	●	●	●	●	●	●	●	●	●			
Squid				●	●	●	●	●	●	●	●	●
Tuna*	●	●	●	●	●	●	●	●	●	●	●	●
MEAT												
Beef	●	●	●	●	●	●	●	●	●	●	●	●
Lamb (spring)		●	●	●	●	●	●			●	●	●
Pork	●	●	●	●	●	●	●	●	●	●	●	●
POULTRY & GAME												
Chicken	●	●	●	●	●	●	●	●	●	●	●	●
Duck	●	●	●	●	●	●	●	●	●	●	●	●
Goose							●	●	●	●	●	●
Pheasant								●	●	●	●	●
Quail	●	●	●	●	●	●	●	●	●	●	●	●
Turkey	●	●	●				●	●	●	●	●	●
VEGETABLES & SALADS												
Asparagus			●	●								
Aubergines					●	●	●					
Beans, broad				●	●	●	●					
Beans, French				●	●	●	●	●				
Beans, runner				●	●	●	●	●	●			
Beetroot	●				●	●	●	●	●	●	●	●
Brussels sprouts	●							●	●	●	●	●
Butternut squash							●	●	●	●	●	●
Cabbage (green)	●	●	●	●	●	●	●	●	●	●	●	●
Cabbage (red)	●	●	●	●			●	●	●	●	●	●
Cabbage (Savoy)	●	●	●				●	●	●	●	●	●
Cabbage (white)	●	●	●	●	●	●	●	●	●	●	●	●
Carrots	●	●	●	●	●	●	●	●	●	●	●	●
Celery	●	●	●			●	●	●	●	●	●	●
Chillies					●	●	●	●				
Courgettes				●	●	●	●	●				
Cucumber	●	●	●	●	●	●	●	●	●	●		
Fennel				●	●	●	●	●				

This is an approximate guide to availability since weather conditions vary from region to region. With the exception of items marked as imported, with an asterisk, the chart shows the seasons for produce grown in the UK and northern Europe. The seasons for fish and shellfish apply to wild rather than farmed food.

	SPRING			SUMMER			AUTUMN			WINTER		
	EARLY	MID	LATE	EARLY	MID	LATE	EARLY	MID	LATE	EARLY	MID	LATE
Garlic (fresh)			●	●	●							
Globe artichokes				●	●	●	●	●	●			
Jerusalem artichokes	●							●	●	●	●	●
Leeks	●	●				●	●	●	●	●	●	●
Lettuce			●	●	●	●						
Mushrooms (wild)			●				●	●	●			
Onions (main crop)	●			●	●	●	●	●	●	●	●	
Onions (pickling)				●	●							
Onions (spring)	●	●		●	●	●	●	●	●	●	●	
Parsnips	●						●	●	●	●	●	
Peas				●	●	●	●	●	●			
Peppers				●	●	●	●	●				
Potatoes	●	●	●	●	●	●	●	●	●	●	●	
Pumpkin							●	●	●			
Rocket		●	●	●	●	●	●	●	●	●	●	
Shallots	●						●	●	●	●	●	
Spinach	●	●	●	●	●	●	●	●	●	●	●	
Swede	●						●	●	●	●	●	
Sweetcorn					●	●	●	●				
Sweet potato*	●	●	●				●	●	●	●	●	
Tomatoes					●	●	●	●				
Turnip (baby)			●	●			●	●	●	●	●	
Watercress	●	●	●	●	●	●	●	●	●	●	●	
HERBS												
Basil			●	●	●	●	●					
Chives		●	●	●	●	●	●	●	●			
Coriander		●	●	●	●	●	●	●	●			
Dill			●	●	●	●	●					
Mint		●	●	●	●	●	●	●	●			
Oregano		●	●	●	●	●	●	●	●	●	●	●
Parsley (curly)	●	●	●	●	●	●	●	●	●	●	●	●
Parsley (flat leaf)		●	●	●	●	●	●	●	●	●	●	●
Rosemary	●	●	●	●	●	●	●	●	●	●	●	●
Sage	●	●	●	●	●	●	●	●	●	●	●	●
Tarragon			●	●	●	●	●	●				
Thyme		●	●	●	●	●	●	●	●	●		
FRUIT & NUTS												
Apples	●						●	●	●	●	●	●
Apricots*				●	●	●	●					
Almonds*									●	●	●	●
Blackberries				●	●	●	●					
Blueberries				●	●	●						
Cherries				●	●	●						
Cranberries*								●	●	●		
Grapes*	●	●	●	●	●	●	●	●	●	●	●	●
Oranges	●	●	●	●	●	●	●	●	●	●	●	●
Pears							●	●	●	●	●	●
Raspberries				●	●	●	●	●				
Rhubarb	●	●	●	●	●	●					●	●
Strawberries				●	●	●	●					

CONVERSION CHARTS

OVEN TEMPERATURES

CELSIUS	FAHRENHEIT	GAS MARK	OVEN HEAT
110°	225°	¼	very cool
120°	250°	½	very cool
140°	275°	1	cool
150°	300°	2	cool
160°	325°	3	moderate
180°	350°	4	moderate
190°	375°	5	moderately hot
200°	400°	6	moderately hot
220°	425°	7	hot
230°	450°	8	very hot
240°	475°	9	very hot

SPOON MEASUREMENTS

1 teaspoon of liquid = 5 ml

1 tablespoon of liquid = 15 ml

OTHER MEASUREMENTS

Liquid volume

Metric	Imperial
50 ml	2 fl oz
100 ml	3½ fl oz
150 ml	5 fl oz
200 ml	7 fl oz
300 ml	10 fl oz
450 ml	16 fl oz
500 ml	18 fl oz
600 ml	1 pint
700 ml	1¼ pints
850 ml	1½ pints
1 litre	1¾ pints
1.5 litres	2¾ pints
2.8 litres	5 pints
3 litres	5¼ pints

Weight

Metric	Imperial
5 g	⅛ oz
10 g	¼ oz
25 g	1 oz
50 g	1¾ oz
75 g	2¾ oz
85 g	3 oz
100 g	3½ oz
150 g	5½ oz
225 g	8 oz
300 g	10½ oz
450 g	1 lb
500 g	1 lb 2 oz
1 kg	2 lb 4 oz
1.5 kg	3 lb 5 oz

Linear

Metric	Imperial
2 mm	1/16 inch
3 mm	⅛ inch
5 mm	¼ inch
8 mm	⅜ inch
1 cm	½ inch
2 cm	¾ inch
2.5 cm	1 inch
5 cm	2 inches
7.5 cm	3 inches
10 cm	4 inches
20 cm	8 inches
30 cm	12 inches/1 foot
46 cm	18 inches/1½ feet
50 cm	20 inches/1⅔ feet

PREPARATION TECHNIQUES

You will find this section a valuable source of reference for all the basic preparation techniques you are likely to need in everyday cooking. There are also some advanced techniques for the more experienced cook.

GRIND

This term means to crush food, such as nuts or coffee beans, to a powder or into very small pieces. For this job, you can use a coffee grinder or food processor, or a pestle and mortar for a coarser result.

INFUSE

This technique involves steeping flavourful ingredients, such as herbs or spices, in a liquid in order to flavour it.

BARD

This means to wrap pieces of fat, such as bacon, around lean cuts of meat and poultry.

CRUSH

This technique is useful for bringing out the flavour of garlic and herbs.

BASTE

When you spoon juices or fat over food during cooking, this is known as 'basting'. It helps to keep the food moist and seal in the flavour.

FOLD

This involves mixing a light mixture into a heavier one using a spoon or spatula in a figure-of-eight movement. This is done to keep the air within the mixture.

MARINATE

This term means to soak food in a marinade for a few hours or days to tenderize it and give it more flavour. You can marinate meat, poultry, fish and vegetables.

BEAT

This technique involves using a fork, spoon or electric mixer in a vigorous stirring motion to remove any lumps from sauces and incorporate air into omelettes and cake mixtures.

DEGLAZE

After the food and excess fat have been removed from the pan, a small amount of liquid – such as stock or wine – is stirred in to loosen browned bits of food in the pan. This is called deglazing.

KNOCK BACK

This entails knocking the air out of bread dough after it has risen.

RUB IN

This is used mainly for pastry making. Using fingertips, the fat is rubbed into the flour, lifting it high over the basin in order to trap air into the mixture.

GRIND

CRUSH

FOLD

RUB IN

WHISK

SHRED

CHIFFONADE

CLARIFY

You can clarify butter or a liquid. To clarify butter, heat it slowly to separate the milk solids, which sink to the bottom of the pan, skimming any foam off the top. To clarify a liquid, such as a stock, add egg whites and/or egg shells to it and simmer for 10 minutes, then cool and strain it. The egg whites or shells draw out the impurities.

SHRED

This technique involves using a small, sharp knife or grater to cut food into very thin lengths.

LINE

This means lining a tin with something to prevent food sticking to it during cooking. The most common method is to rub butter or oil over the inner surface of the tin, or to cover it with baking parchment before adding the food.

KNEAD

This technique uses the heel of the hand to pull and stretch bread dough in order to develop the gluten in the flour so that the bread will keep its shape when it has risen. You can also knead dough in a food processor or food mixer that has a dough hook attachment.

WHISK

Whisking involves beating a light mixture, such as cream and eggs, vigorously with a whisk to incorporate more air. You can use a balloon whisk (but it takes a lot of effort), an electric hand mixer, a free-standing mixer or a food processor with a whisk attachment.

SKIM

This term means to remove foam or fat from the surface of a simmering liquid with a large slotted spoon or a ladle.

ZEST

This means to remove the outer layer of a citrus fruit skin without the bitter pith.

CHIFFONADE

A French term meaning 'made of rags', it refers to the effect you get when you roll leafy vegetables together, then slice them crossways with a sharp knife to make ribbons.

ENRICH

This means adding a rich ingredient to a dish in order to create a richer texture or flavour. For example, you could add butter to a dough, or cream to a sauce.

GLAZE

This involves brushing water, beaten egg, or sugar and water onto pastry before baking to give it a glossy shine (and make it crunchy if sugar is added).

EMULSIFY

Emulsification happens when one liquid is slowly added to another in a gradual stream while stirring or blending rapidly. For example, mayonnaise is made by adding oil in a slow stream to a beaten egg mixture while whisking or blending.

EMULSIFY

LARD

To lard means to insert strips of pork fat into a lean cut of meat to flavour it and keep it moist.

JULIENNE

This technique involves cutting food, such as carrots and celery, into fine batons or strips.

TENDERIZE

This involves pounding meat, such as a beef steak, with a mallet in order to break down the tough fibres. You can also tenderize meat by marinating it.

GREASE OR OIL

This is to rub a little butter or oil over the surface of a pan or tin to prevent food sticking to it during cooking.

STEEP

Steeping means to soak an ingredient in hot liquid in order to release its flavour into the liquid.

CUT

This method means to use a sharp knife to make an incision or separate a food into smaller pieces.

MASH

This means to reduce cooked food (usually potatoes or other root vegetables) to a pulp using a potato masher or ricer.

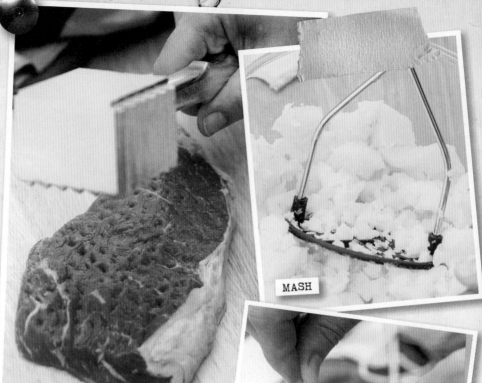

TENDERIZE

MASH

TRUSS

CHOP

This means to cut food into small pieces using a sharp knife. For example, to chop a herb, hold the tip of the knife blade down with one hand, then use your other hand to raise the handle of the knife up and down as you chop the herb. You can chop food roughly or finely, depending on your requirements. Roughly chopped means that the food will be left in larger pieces.

DRESS

This can mean to add a dressing to a salad, to decorate a dish before serving or to pluck and truss poultry.

TRUSS

This means to pull a poultry or game bird into shape then secure with string or skewers before cooking. This technique is particularly useful for preventing stuffing falling out of a bird.

CREAM

Creaming is similar to beating, in that you use a fork, spoon or electric mixer to beat ingredients together until they are smooth. This technique is usually associated with something rich and creamy, such as butter.

PURÉE

This describes reducing food to a smooth pulp. You can do this by pushing food through a sieve or using a blender.

MACERATE

To macerate means to soak a food in a liquid, often alcohol, to soften it.

OPEN FREEZE

This technique means to freeze foods, uncovered, in a single layer. For example, you can cut fruit, such as mango, into small pieces, spread them out on a tray and freeze them uncovered. Then transfer the pieces individually to a freezer bag and use as required.

CRIMP

For this technique, use the finger and thumb of one hand and the index finger of the other hand to 'pinch' pastry together around the edge of a pie or pasty. This gives it a decorative effect.

CURE

Curing means to preserve a food by salting or smoking it.

DEGORGE

This is soaking meat, poultry or fish in a solution of cold water and salt to remove impurities. This term is also used for salting aubergines to remove their bitter juices.

DREDGE

This means to sprinkle flour onto a surface when rolling pastry, or icing sugar or cocoa powder over desserts.

SIFT

This technique involves shaking dry ingredients, such as flour, through a sieve to remove lumps and introduce more air into the mixture.

MINCE

This is to grind food, such as meat, into small pieces using a knife or mincer.

CROSS-HATCH

To cross-hatch means to score criss-cross patterns on the surface of foods to allow them to absorb marinades or be removed from their skins. You can cross-hatch the outer layer of fat on a pork joint before cooking to allow the fat to drain and create a decorative effect.

GRATE

This means to shred food into small pieces. You can use a box grater or food processor.

SHUCK

This term refers to removing the husks from corn and the shells from peas.

SNIP

This means using kitchen scissors to cut green leafy vegetables or herbs into very small pieces.

SIFT

CROSS HATCH

PURÉE

EGGS & DAIRY

Nowadays we can buy a wide range of delicious eggs which are full of protein and very easy to prepare and cook. Likewise, more dairy products are available than ever before and we can choose from an ever-increasing array of milk, yogurt, cream, butter and cheese.

BUYING & STORING EGGS

Always buy your eggs from a reputable supplier, and do not buy any with cracked shells. Ensure the eggs are as fresh as possible by checking the 'best before' date on the carton. In many cases the 'best before' date is also printed on the eggshells themselves. You can also check an egg's freshness by floating it in water: if it sinks to the bottom of the bowl horizontally, it is very fresh; if it stays vertical with its tip on the bottom, it is less fresh; if it floats to the top, it is stale and should be discarded. Store your eggs, pointed ends down, in their carton at the back of a low shelf in the refrigerator. They should not be stored in the refrigerator door, where they will be subject to fluctuations in temperature each time the door is opened. Separated egg whites will keep in the refrigerator in a lidded container for a week, and in the freezer for three months. Always label the container with the date of freezing and what it contains. Eggs are best cooked from room temperature, so remember to take them out of the refrigerator about an hour before they are needed.

WHISKING EGG WHITES

Eggs that are 3–5 days old are best for whisking. Make sure that everything is clean and that your bowl is free of grease. Put the egg whites in a large bowl. If whisking by hand, use a large balloon whisk in an upward, circular movement. Alternatively, use a hand-held electric whisk or free-standing food mixer. If the recipe calls for a 'soft peaks' consistency, the mixture should form peaks that will flop over when the whisk is removed. If you need 'firm peaks', the peaks should stand rigid.

KNOWING YOUR EGGS

COLL DUCK EGG

GOOSE EGG

QUAIL EGG

AYLESBURY DUCK EGG

FREE-RANGE HEN EGG

KHAKI CAMPBELL DUCK EGG

SCRAMBLING EGGS

Allow 2 eggs and 1 tablespoon of milk per person. Whisk together the eggs and milk in a bowl, then season with salt and pepper. Melt 1 tablespoon of butter in a non-stick pan, then pour in the egg mixture. Stir constantly over a low heat for 5–7 minutes until almost set, then remove from the heat. Stir for 1 more minute, then serve.

BOILING EGGS

To boil eggs, bring a small saucepan of water to the boil. Reduce the heat to a simmer, add a pinch of salt, then carefully add the

SEPARATING EGGS

There are some clever devices available for separating yolks from egg whites, but if you don't have a separating gadget, you can use the shell method (using cold eggs makes this method easier). 1 Crack the egg shell gently on the edge of a bowl. 2 Open the shell slowly, allowing the white to drip into the bowl. 3 Taking care not to break the yolk, pass it from one shell half to the other. 4 Repeat until the yolk and white are fully separated. Alternatively, open the egg into your hand, cradling the yolk gently, and let the white drip through your fingers to separate.

eggs. Simmer gently for 4–5 minutes for soft-boiled, and 9–10 minutes for hard-boiled (no longer, or a dark ring will appear around the yolk). Remove with a slotted spoon and plunge into cold water to prevent further cooking. Serve as required.

FRYING EGGS

Heat 1–2 tablespoons of oil in a frying pan until hot (but not smoking). Break the eggs carefully into the pan so that the yolks remain intact. Cook over a medium heat, occasionally basting with the hot oil to help the yolk set, for 3–4 minutes. Use a fish slice to lift out the eggs and allow the oil to drain away.

POACHING EGGS

Eggs need to be very fresh for poaching or they will break up in the water. You can use a non-stick egg poacher or silicone poaching pods for this, or alternatively you can use the following method.

Fill a small frying pan with enough water to cover an egg. Bring to the boil, then reduce the heat to a simmer. Break the egg carefully into a cup, then pour it gently into the boiling water so that the yolk does not break. Cook for 3–4 minutes; you can baste the egg with a little of the cooking liquid to ensure it is cooked. Lift it out with a slotted spoon and serve.

CODDLING EGGS

An egg coddler is a porcelain cup with a lid. Grease the coddler with butter, break an egg into it, season wth salt and pepper and loosely screw on the lid. Meanwhile, bring a saucepan of water to the boil, stand the coddler in the water up to the bottom of its lid and simmer for 7–8 minutes. Remove and serve.

SAFETY
Eggs can carry harmful bacteria and may cause food poisoning if not thoroughly cooked, so do not give dishes with raw or lightly cooked eggs to people who may be particularly vulnerable, such as pregnant or breastfeeding women, babies and toddlers, the elderly, people who are ill or convalescents.

KNOWING YOUR DAIRY

MILK

YOGURT

BUTTER

CHEDDAR

PARMESAN

CURD CHEESE

STILTON

CLOTTED CREAM

BUYING & STORING MILK

Milk is a good source of protein and calcium. The most commonly available is fresh cow's milk, which comes in full-fat (4% fat), semi-skimmed (less than 2% fat) and skimmed (less than 1% fat). Other varieties include homogenized, which has the fat spread throughout the milk so that there is no creamy layer on top, and long-life (UHT) milk, which has been heated quickly to around 149°C/300°F, then cooled and vacuum-packed to ensure a shelf-life without refrigeration of around six months. You can also buy condensed milk, which is very thick and sweet; evaporated milk, which is sterilized in tins and often used to replace full-fat milk; buttermilk, which tastes like yogurt or thickened low-fat milk; and powdered milk, which you can reconstitute with water and use in place of fresh milk. If you are sensitive to cow's milk, you can buy goat's milk or sheep's milk, or milk made from soya or rice instead.

Most fresh milk is pasteurized (heated then quickly cooled) in order to kill off any harmful bacteria, although some unpasteurized milk is available, often straight from the farm (see Safety box, below). Always check the 'best before' date on milk before you buy it, and store fresh milk, covered, in the refrigerator. Semi-skimmed and skimmed milk can be frozen for up to 3 weeks.

BUYING & STORING YOGURT

Yogurt is made by fermenting milk with healthy bacteria. It has a slightly tangy taste and is a healthy choice because it is thick and creamy yet low in fat. Greek-style yogurt is the thickest and has the creamiest consistency. You can also freeze yogurt for a healthy low-fat alternative to ice cream. Check the 'best before' date before buying, and store it in the refrigerator. Keep it covered when not in use.

BUYING & STORING BUTTER

Butter is made by churning cream until it separates into semi-solids. It comprises at least 80% fat and the other 20% is made up of milk solids and water. Sometimes it is coloured with annatto (a natural colour made from the paste of seeds). Butter is available in salted and unsalted varieties: unsalted is essential for sweet dishes. You can also buy 'spreadable' butter: this has been blended with oil so that it will stay soft and can be spread more easily. Make sure your butter is always tightly wrapped to

prevent it absorbing odours. Check the 'best before' date on the packaging. Butter also freezes well, for up to 6 months in the freezer.

BUYING & STORING CREAM

Cream is made from the fattiest part of milk. It therefore has a higher fat content than milk, and a milder flavour. Half-fat and single cream have the lowest fat content: the former is useful for pouring into drinks such as coffee, and the latter is ideal for sauces and soups. Soured cream (around 18–20% fat) has a slightly tangy taste and is ideal in savoury dishes, as is the higher fat crème fraîche (up to 50% fat). Whipping cream has a high fat content (30–35%) and is ideal for whipping and piping into decorative shapes. Double cream has a very high fat content (over 40%) and should therefore be used sparingly. It is a delicious luxury for special occasions, perhaps to enrich a sauce or accompany a dessert. Double cream can be frozen for up to 3 weeks. Clotted cream has the highest fat content of all (around 60%) and is very thick. It is ideal on scones or as an accompaniment for special desserts. All cream should be kept covered, stored in the refrigerator and used by the 'best before' date on the carton.

BUYING & STORING CHEESE

Cheese is made from milk that is allowed to thicken and then separate into curds (semi-solids) and whey (a liquid). Fresh cheeses are rindless and vary in consistency. Typical cheeses in this category are cream cheese and cottage cheese. Soft and semi-hard cheeses are firmer, and range from creamy soft cheeses with rinds, such as Brie, to firmer cheeses such as Port Salut. Generally, the harder the cheese, the higher the fat content, and hard cheeses have the highest fat of all. They are often easy to grate, and range from Cheddar cheese to Parmesan. Blue cheeses are also available: these have blue veins running through them and a strong flavour and aroma (the veins are made by a friendly bacteria). Blue cheese varieties include Gorgonzola and Stilton. You can also buy cheese made from goat's milk and sheep's milk.

Keep your cheese tightly wrapped. Store fresh cheese in the coldest part of the refrigerator, and the other cheeses in the warmest part. Hard cheeses can be grated ready for use and kept in the refrigerator for up to one week. Use cheeses by the 'best before' date. You can also freeze hard cheeses, but they will have a crumblier texture when they are defrosted. Grated cheese also freezes well but is then only suitable for cooking, not for adding to salads.

SAFETY
Unpasteurized milk is available from specialist suppliers, but there is still a risk of disease and therefore this milk should not be given to vulnerable people, especially pregnant or breastfeeding women, babies and toddlers, the elderly, people who are ill or convalescents.

MEAT

Meat is rich in protein and easy to cook. It makes an excellent centrepiece to any meal, and you can choose from a wide range of joints and cuts, from the economical to the indulgent, to suit any occasion.

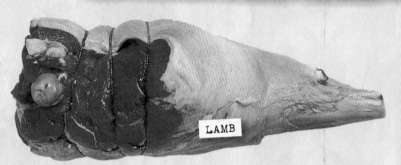

LAMB

BEEF

BUYING & STORING MEAT

Always buy your fresh meat from a reputable supplier. For lamb, choose firm, pinkish, marbled meat; avoid any that looks dark and soggy. The fat should be cream-coloured. For pork, choose moist, pinkish meat with white fat. Avoid any meat that looks oily or that has yellow fat. For beef, look for meat that is deep burgundy red, the fat should be cream-coloured. Choose beef that has a marbling of fat through it – this will ensure that the meat stays moist during cooking. If you are buying a joint of meat, allow 175–350 g/ 6–12 oz per person, depending on whether the meat is on or off the bone. Once you get the meat home, unwrap it and transfer it to a clean dish (the dish should have a lip deep enough to catch any juices). Cover with clingfilm and store in the refrigerator away from any cooked meats. Leave any prepackaged meat in its wrapping in the refrigerator and use by the 'best before' date. Unpackaged minced lamb, beef and pork is best used within 1–2 days of purchase. Fresh cuts of beef and pork will keep in the refrigerator for 2–3 days, and cooked beef and pork can be refrigerated for 4–5 days. Fresh lamb cuts will keep for up to 4 days in the refrigerator. Before cooking, bring out the meat and allow it to come back to room temperature for about 30 minutes. You can freeze small cuts of beef or pork for up to 6 months, and lamb for up to 3 months. Make sure you thaw the meat thoroughly in a refrigerator or cool room before cooking: allow 6 hours per 450 g/1 lb.

PREPARATION TECHNIQUES

There is a range of techniques you can use to prepare and/or improve your chosen cuts of meat before cooking. Some of them are done purely for presentation, while other techniques help to tenderize the meat or facilitate thorough cooking.

LAMB CHOPS

Use a sharp knife to remove the excess fat around the edge.

PORK CHOPS & RUMP STEAKS

Use a sharp knife to make incisions in the fat at intervals of 2.5 cm/1 inch around the edge. This helps prevent the meat curling up at the sides during cooking.

BRAISING STEAK

Remove excess fat with a sharp knife. Slice across the grain and cut across the slices to form cubes.

PORK

TENDERIZE THIN CUTS OF MEAT

Put the meat between sheets of greaseproof paper and pound with either a meat mallet or the base of a saucepan.

STUFF & TIE A BONELESS JOINT

Put it skin-side down and arrange the stuffing evenly over the surface. Roll up the joint from the thick end, tie a piece of clean string lengthways around the joint, then knot it and trim off the ends. Tie further pieces of string crossways around the joint at intervals of about 2.5 cm/1 inch. Knot each one in turn and trim the ends.

BUTTERFLY A LEG OF LAMB

Push a chef's knife into the cavity of the bone, then cut sideways to part the meat. Open it out and make a light incision down the centre of the meat so that it stays open and flat.

PREPARE A RACK OF LAMB

Remove the skin and excess fat, leaving a layer of fat about 15 mm/⅝ inch thick. Cut off the bone at the back, then remove the fat from the ends of the bones (to a length of about 5 cm/ 2 inches). Use a knife to scrape out the meat from between the bones.

CHOOSING CUTS OF MEAT

There are many different cuts of meat available. Choosing the right cut will help to ensure the perfect result for your chosen recipe. When in doubt, ask your local butcher for advice.

BEEF

For roasting, choose sirloin, topside fillet or rib. Fillet and steaks are excellent for grilling, pan-frying or barbecuing. For braising and stewing, use chuck, topside fillet or rib.

PORK

For roasting, choose the belly, leg, loin, shoulder, fillet, chops or steaks. For grilling, use the belly, escalopes, loin, shoulder, fillet, chops or steaks. The belly, loin, fillet, chops or steaks are excellent for barbecues. For frying, use the loin, fillet, chops and steaks, and also bacon. To stew or braise, use the leg, shoulder or loin.

VEAL

The breast, loin and shoulder are best for roasting, while the loin, topside and cutlets are ideal for grilling and barbecuing. For pan-frying, choose the loin or topside, and for stewing or braising use the knuckle, shoulder or breast.

LAMB

The leg is the most popular choice for roasting, but you can also roast the shoulder, saddle, breast and best end of neck. For grilling, try chops, noisettes, leg and best end of neck. The leg or chops are ideal for barbecues, and for pan-frying use noisettes or the middle neck. Finally, for stewing, braising or casseroles, use the shoulder, shank or middle neck.

COOKING & CARVING TECHNIQUES

Techniques for cooking and carving joints of meat are not difficult, but they do have to be performed properly in order to get the best out of the meat. Follow the instructions given here for perfect results every time.

ROASTING & CARVING A BONED JOINT

This technique is suitable for boned joints of lamb, pork and beef. Rub the surface with a little oil, followed by some salt and some crushed peppercorns (use a pestle and mortar for this). Place on a rack in a roasting tin, then roast in the oven, basting once or twice during cooking. Remove from the oven and cut off the strings. Wrap the meat in foil and leave to stand for 15–20 minutes. To carve, steady the meat with a fork, then carve slices downwards from one end.

ROASTING & CARVING A LEG OF LAMB

Using a sharp knife, score a criss-cross pattern in the fat, then rub all over the surface with a little oil, followed by some salt and freshly ground black pepper. Put the meat on a rack in a roasting tin and roast in the oven, basting once or twice during cooking. To test if the meat is cooked all the way through, pierce a skewer or knife into the thickest part. The juices that run out will be clear if the meat is cooked. If not, return it to the oven and cook until it is done. Remove from the oven and wrap the meat in foil. Leave to stand for 15–20 minutes. To carve, turn the leg meat-side up, then steady the meat with a fork. Start carving from the knuckle end. When you have finished, turn over the leg and carve horizontal slices.

USING A MEAT THERMOMETER

A meat thermometer is a useful device for testing whether a joint of meat is cooked thoroughly. Thorough cooking is particularly important in the case of pork, which can carry harmful bacteria and cause food poisoning if not cooked all the way through. Simply insert the thermometer into the thickest part of the meat at the start of cooking. Take care to ensure that the thermometer does not come into contact with any bone, because this could give a false reading. When the thermometer reaches the required temperature, the meat is cooked. The recommended temperatures for different meats are shown on the next page.

OVEN TEMPERATURES & ROASTING TIMES

Please note that individual oven temperatures and cooking times vary, so the following cooking times are approximate only. Remember to preheat the oven before cooking in order to ensure the best results.

MEAT	JOINT	WEIGHT	TEMPERATURE	COOKING TIME
LAMB	Whole leg	2.5 kg/5 lb 8 oz	180°C/350°F/Gas Mark 4	2¼ hours (medium rare) or 2½ hours (well done)
LAMB	Whole shoulder	2.5 kg /5 lb 8 oz	180°C/350°F/Gas Mark 4	2¼ hours (medium rare) or 2½ hours (well done)
PORK	Loin (boned)	2.5 kg/5 lb 8 oz	180°C/350°F/Gas Mark 4 220°C/425°F/Gas Mark 7	3 hours at lower temperature, then 20 minutes at higher temperature (well done)
PORK	Shoulder (boned)	2.5 kg/5 lb 8 oz	180°C/350°F/Gas Mark 4 220°C/425°F/Gas Mark 7	3 hours at lower temperature, then 20 minutes at higher temperature (well done)
BEEF	Sirloin	2.5 kg/5 lb 8 oz	200°C/400°F/Gas Mark 6	1¾ hours (rare), 2¼ hours (medium rare) or 2½ hours (well done)
BEEF	Topside	2 kg/4 lb 8 oz	180°C/350°F/Gas Mark 4	1½ hours (rare), 2 hours (medium rare) or 2½ hours (well done)

OVEN TEMPERATURES & HEAT DESCRIPTIONS

You may come across recipes that do not give a specific temperature: instead they will simply recommend cooking in a 'moderate' or 'hot' oven. Here is a list of these heat descriptions and their correct temperatures.

OVEN HEAT DESCRIPTION	CELSIUS	FAHRENHEIT	GAS MARK
VERY COOL	110–120°	225–250°	¼–½
COOL	140–150°	275–300°	1–2
MODERATE	160–180°	325–350°	3–4
MODERATELY HOT	190–200°	375–400°	5–6
HOT	220°	425°	7
VERY HOT	230–240°	450–475°	8–9

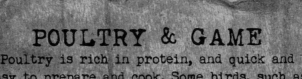

POULTRY & GAME

Poultry is rich in protein, and quick and easy to prepare and cook. Some birds, such as chicken and turkey, can be a low-fat choice as long as the fatty skin is removed, and they are very versatile. Duck is fattier, but makes a good dinner-party choice.

BUYING & STORING POULTRY AND GAME

Always buy your poultry and game as fresh as possible and from a reputable supplier. Choose plump birds that have unblemished skin, and make sure that any wrapping or packaging is intact.

As soon as you get it home, remove the packaging (if it is a fresh bird) and transfer the giblets (if any) to a separate bowl. Place the bird on a rack in a dish, then cover it and any giblets loosely with clingfilm and store in the refrigerator. Keep it well away from cooked meats to prevent any cross-contamination. Whole birds will keep for 1–2 days in the refrigerator, and giblets no longer than 1 day. Frozen birds can be stored in the freezer in their orignal packaging. Thaw in the refrigerator thoroughly before cooking: you will need to allow 5 hours per 450 g/1 lb for a chicken and 6 hours per 450 g/1 lb for a turkey. Game birds are available fresh when in season and frozen all year round. If they are truly wild birds and not farmed, they will have a lower fat content and should therefore be wrapped in bacon or pork fat during roasting. Older birds are not recommended for roasting – they are more suited to soups, casseroles and stews. Game animals, such as venison and rabbit, tend to be less tender than farmed animals because they get more exercise in the wild. They should therefore be cooked slowly until tender, but not overcooked. Braising is a good method for keeping the meat moist, or it can be roasted if wrapped first in bacon or pork fat.

TYPES OF BIRD

In addition to the flavour, the choice of bird may depend on the occasion and how many people you are catering for.

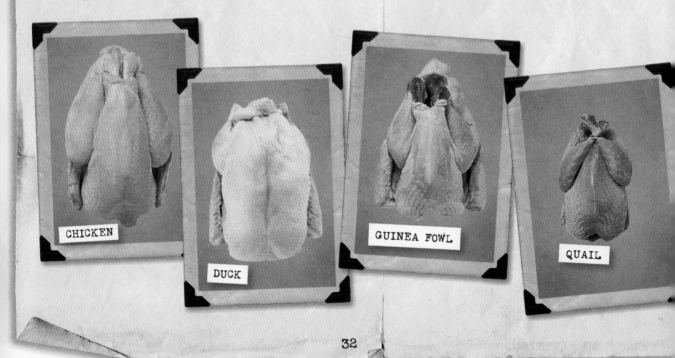

CHICKEN

DUCK

GUINEA FOWL

QUAIL

CHICKEN

There are many different varieties of chicken available, including free range, organic and corn-fed. You can buy whole birds ready prepared for the oven or frozen. You can also buy a variety of joints – wing, breast, leg, thigh or drumstick – or you can joint a whole bird yourself. Chicken is delicious roasted, steamed, poached, grilled, casseroled, barbecued, chargrilled, stir-fried, pan-fried or deep-fried.

POUSSIN

A poussin is a very young, small chicken. Poussins weigh up to 450 g/1 lb and you should therefore allow one whole bird per person. They are suitable for roasting, barbecuing and grilling.

GUINEA FOWL

This bird is related to the chicken and the partridge, and has light and dark meat and a strong flavour. It is available fresh and frozen. Since guinea fowl has a low fat content, it is most suited to moist cooking methods such as casseroling. Alternatively, you can wrap it in bacon rashers or pork fat and roast it.

TURKEY

These birds are much larger than chickens – some can grow to a massive 31.5 kg/ 70 lb – but the trend nowadays is for much smaller birds. This is because turkey suppliers would like to encourage their use all year round, rather than just during Christmas and other holiday periods. Turkeys have similar uses to chickens, and you can often interchange them with chickens in recipes. You can buy whole birds ready prepared for the oven or frozen. You can also buy separate joints, such as breast joints or drumsticks. Turkey is particularly suitable for roasting, casseroling, braising, stir-frying or pan-frying.

DUCK

Ducks are available whole, fresh and frozen. Breast and leg joints are also available. Duck is fattier than chicken or turkey, and is therefore particularly suitable for roasting, grilling or pan-frying. Duck is often served with a tart fruit sauce.

PARTRIDGE

This game bird has dark flesh and an earthy flavour. Its flesh can be tough so is best braised, stewed or casseroled. It can also be roasted.

GOOSE

Geese are larger than ducks, and can be bought fresh, although they are more often bought frozen. Although they are popular during holidays and at Christmas time, especially in Europe, they have become less popular year-round because of their very high fat content. Geese are best roasted, pot-roasted, braised or stewed. It is also a good idea to serve them with a tart fruit sauce in order to cut through any fatty aftertaste.

PHEASANT

These are medium-sized game birds. The male has more brilliant plumage than the female, but the female is juicier and more tender. Young pheasants can be roasted, but older birds should be wrapped in bacon or pork fat during roasting; they can also be braised, casseroled or stewed.

QUAIL

These small game birds are related to the partridge. The European variety has lean, medium-dark flesh, whereas the American variety has lean but lighter flesh. Both types have a sweet flavour. Quails are suitable for roasting, pot-roasting, braising, barbecuing, casseroling or grilling. Their small eggs have a speckled brown shell and a rich flavour.

VENISON

Deer is a popular game animal and the meat is available wild or farmed. It is low in cholesterol, and usually available as leg or saddle joints, or as steaks. The best meat comes from a male deer under the age of two years. Venison meat is quite dry and is therefore more suited to casseroles.

PREPARATION & COOKING TECHNIQUES

It is essential to cook poultry all the way through in order to kill off any potentially harmful bacteria. If a bird is not cooked through when tested, return it to the oven to finish cooking, even if you have to exceed the recommended cooking time.

MAKING CHICKEN STOCK

Chicken stock is easy to prepare and is ideal for adding to soups and sauces. It can be stored, covered with clingfilm, in the refrigerator for 2–3 days. You can also freeze it for up to 6 months. Put the chicken carcass into a large saucepan with 1 chopped onion, 1 sliced carrot, 1 chopped celery stick and 1 chopped leek. Add 1 bay leaf and 1 sprig of thyme, 3 stalks of parsley and some cracked black peppercorns. Cover with water and bring to the boil, then use a slotted spoon to skim off any scum from the surface. Reduce the heat, cover, and leave to simmer for 2–3 hours. Strain into a large bowl and discard the solids. Use the stock as required.

ROASTING A LARGE CHICKEN OR A TURKEY

First wipe the bird inside and out with kitchen paper. If you are going to stuff it, pull back the skin around the neck cavity and insert the stuffing into the neck end only (do not overfill the bird or it will not cook through properly). If you are not stuffing the bird, simply season the cavity. Pull the skin over the top, then pull up the wings and tie with string. Pull the legs together and tie with string. Rub butter or oil over the skin of the bird, then season to taste with salt and pepper. Transfer to a wire rack in a roasting tin, and roast in a preheated oven, basting occasionally, until cooked through and tender. To test, insert a sharp knife or skewer into the thickest part of the bird: if the juices run clear, the bird is cooked. If not, return it to the oven and cook until done. Remove from the oven and leave to rest, covered in foil, for 15–20 minutes before carving.

ROASTING A GOOSE

Wipe the goose inside and out with kitchen paper and pull out any excess fat from inside. Season well with salt and pepper. If you are going to stuff the goose insert the stuffing as far as possible in the neck flap end, securing the flap with a skewer. Prick the goose all over with a fork, lay on a rack in a roasting tin and place in a preheated oven. To test that it is cooked all the way through, insert a skewer into the thickest part of the bird: if the juices run clear, the bird is cooked. Remove from the oven and leave to rest for 20 minutes before carving.

OVEN TEMPERATURES AND ROASTING TIMES

Individual oven temperatures and cooking times vary, so cooking times are approximate. Preheat the oven before cooking.

BIRD	WEIGHT	TEMPERATURE	COOKING TIME
CHICKEN	3 kg/6 lb 8 oz	200°C/400°F/Gas Mark 6	2¼ hours
TURKEY	5 kg/11 lb	180°C/350°F/Gas Mark 4	3½ hours
	8 kg/18 lb	180°C/350°F/Gas Mark	4¾–5 hours
QUAIL	450 g/1 lb	200°C/400°F/Gas Mark 6	30 minutes
GOOSE	5 kg/11 lb	220°C/425°F/Gas Mark 7	30 minutes at higher temperature,
		180°C/350°F/Gas Mark 4	then for 2–3 hours at lower temperature
DUCK	2.5 kg/5 lb 8 oz	220°C/425°F/Gas Mark 7	20 minutes at higher temperature,
		180°C/350°F/Gas Mark 4	then for 2 hours at lower temperature

CARVING A LARGE BIRD

Place the cooked bird breast-side up on a clean chopping board. Use a carving knife to cut between one wing and the side of the breast. Remove the wing and cut thin, downward slices through the breast meat. Repeat with the other side, reserving the wings and the breast slices. Pull out one leg and cut through the joint. Repeat with the other side. Slice the meat from the thighs and drumsticks. Serve the wings and the meat slices.

ROASTING AND CARVING A DUCK

Wipe the duck inside and out with kitchen paper. Duck has a high fat content, so remove any surplus fat. Season inside the tail cavity and insert a bay leaf. Transfer the bird to a wire rack in a roasting tin. Use a fork to prick holes all over it, then season with salt and pepper. Roast in a preheated oven until cooked through and tender (turn and baste it halfway through the cooking time). To test that the bird is cooked all the way through, insert a sharp knife or skewer into the thickest part of the bird: if the juices run clear, the bird is cooked. To serve the duck, joint it by cutting it in half lengthways. Alternatively, use a sharp knife to separate the legs from the body, then cut off the wings. Remove the breast meat and slice it. Serve the legs, wings and slices of breast meat.

JOINTING A WHOLE BIRD

1 To cut a large raw bird into joints, remove any string and place it on a clean chopping board, breast-side up, with the legs pointing towards you.

2 Using a sharp knife, cut the skin between one leg and the side of the breast, then use your hand to press the leg down flat to the board. Do the same with the other leg. Cut through the joint attaching one of the legs and remove the leg from the body. Do the same for the other side.

3 Turn the bird to face the other way and locate the ridge along the middle of the back. Using a knife, cut away one breast, taking a wing off with it. Do the same with the other breast.

4 To divide the legs into thighs and drumsticks, put them skinside down on the chopping board. Cut through the line to separate the joint. Reserve the carcass for making stock.

HERBS & SPICES

There is a wide range of fresh herbs available all year round in your local supermarket, as well as a tempting array of fragrant and exotic spices. You can also buy frozen herbs, which are a good substitute when fresh herbs are unavailable. It is a good idea to keep some pots of fresh herbs on a windowsill and a selection of dried herbs and spices in your storecupboard.

BUYING & STORING HERBS & SPICES

If you buy fresh herbs as pot plants, place them on a windowsill where they can get plenty of light, and water them regularly. Basil, in particular, needs lots of water, so make sure you do not allow it to dry out. Packaged fresh herbs should be stored in their wrapping in the refrigerator. If you grow herbs in your garden, after picking keep them in a jug of clean water until you are ready to use them. Store dried herbs and ground spices in a cool, dark place – an airy storecupboard is ideal. Use all fresh herbs by their 'best before' date, and go through your storecupboard regularly and throw out any dried herbs and spices that are past their best.

TARRAGON

The dark green pointed leaves of tarragon have an aromatic, aniseed-like flavour. It adds a distinctive flavour to poultry, fish, eggs, sauces, salads and dressings. It is best to use this herb on its own, since its strong flavour can overpower other herbs if mixed with them.

BASIL

There are many species of this herb. It thrives in a warm, Mediterranean climate, and therefore in cold climates it will do better indoors on a windowsill with plenty of sunshine and water. It has a sweet, aromatic flavour, and is particularly good with tomatoes and mozzarella cheese. It is also delicious with poultry, fish and seafood, salads and sauces. This herb is fragile and should therefore be added to recipes towards the end of the cooking time.

THYME

This herb comes in different varieties, and several of them are commonly used in cooking. The leaves add a pungent, aromatic flavour to meat, poultry, egg and potato dishes, and are good in soups, sauces, roasts, casseroles and stews.

OREGANO

This green herb is related to marjoram. It has a pungent flavour and should be used sparingly. It is popular in Italian cooking, particularly on pizzas, and adds an aromatic flavor to meat, poultry, eggs and cheese.

CORIANDER

This pungent herb has bright green leaves and is very popular in Mediterranean and Asian cooking. It adds a distinctive flavour to salads, cooked vegetables and stir-fries.

FENNEL

There are two types of fennel. One has a bulbous base, which can be cooked and used like a vegetable; the other variety has no bulb. Fennel has a strong aniseed flavour. The leaves of both types can be snipped into soups and sauces, and are excellent with fish and egg dishes.

MARJORAM

This ancient herb has pale green leaves and a delicate, sweet flavour. It is ideal with meat, poultry, cheese, tomatoes, eggs, dressings and stir-fries.

ROSEMARY

The silvery, needle-shaped leaves of rosemary have a strong aromatic flavour. It is used in soups, salads, roasts, stuffings, dressings and marinades, as well as on pizzas. The herb also makes delicious skewers for kebabs. It pairs particularly well with potatoes and bread, as well as meat, poultry, fish and eggs.

BAY

The leaves of this aromatic herb come from the Mediterranean laurel tree. The fresh leaves, if you can get them, have more flavour than the dried, but either type will add a good, pungent flavour to soups, sauces, stocks and casseroles. They are usually discarded once the food has absorbed their flavour.

SAGE

This herb has greyish oval leaves and a pungent, slightly bitter taste. It is very common in stuffings, especially those containing onion, and is excellent with pork, poultry, beans, cheese, rice and pasta.

CHERVIL

The dark green, curly leaves of chervil have an aromatic flavour with a hint of aniseed. It is especially good in chicken, fish and egg dishes.

MINT

There are many species of mint, the two best-known being peppermint and spearmint. Peppermint has a more peppery flavour, while spearmint has a fresher mint taste. Mint is a hardy plant and can take over a herb garden if not carefully controlled. Use it to flavour cooked potatoes, peas, sauces, soups, meat dishes, desserts and drinks.

DILL

This herb has feathery green leaves and a mild flavour. Dill is excellent with fish, as well as in salads, cheese dishes and sauces.

CHIVES

These relatives of the onion family have long, hollow stems and edible purple flowers. The fresh stems are snipped into small pieces and added to salads, soups, cream cheese and egg dishes. You can also buy them frozen and dried.

PARSLEY

This versatile herb is rich in vitamins A and C and comes in many varieties. The two most popular types have green leaves that are either curly or flat. Curly parsley is common all year round, while flat-leaf parsley may be found only in some supermarkets and specialist delicatessens. Parsley is used in a wide range of dishes, including soups, salads, sauces, stir-fries and bakes, as well as stuffings, dressings and marinades. It adds a spicy, lingering flavour to meat, poultry, fish, eggs and vegetables, and helps to offset the sulphur aftertaste of garlic. It also makes an attractive garnish, particularly the flat-leaf variety.

TYPES & USES OF SPICES

Spices used to be costly when international travel was comparatively slow and difficult, but now they are less expensive and more widely available.

PAPRIKA

This spice is made from ground red pepper pods and its flavour can vary from mild, sweet and pungent to fiery hot. It is excellent in salads and as a garnish. It also goes well with meat, poultry, eggs, vegetables, cream cheese, pasta, rice and beans.

CARDAMOM

This aromatic spice is related to ginger and has a pungent lemon flavour. You can grind and use the whole pod, or use just the seeds inside. Cardamom is widely used in Asian and Middle Eastern dishes, and adds a distinctive flavour to soups, stews, curries, pastry, bread and cakes.

ALLSPICE

This small berry comes from the West Indies and South America and has a sweet flavour of nutmeg, cinnamon and cloves. You can buy it whole or ground. It is used with meat, onions and fruit desserts, as well as in cakes and bread.

MUSTARD

This hot, acrid spice is available as whole seeds, ground, or processed into a paste that ranges in intensity from mild to strong. It goes well with meat, poultry, seafood, eggs, beans, potatoes, cheese, cream and butter sauces, bread, marinades, chutneys and relishes.

CHILLI POWDER

This powdered mixture of spices includes dried chillies, cumin, coriander and cloves. It has a fiery heat but you can also buy mild chilli powder. Use it to flavour soups and stews. It goes well with seafood, meat, poultry, vegetables, beans and eggs.

FENNEL SEEDS

You can buy fennel seeds whole or ground. They have a sweet, mildly aniseed flavour and can be used in savoury and sweet dishes, including marinades, pizzas, stuffings, bread, cakes, biscuits and a variety of desserts and drinks.

STAR ANISE

This star-shaped brown pod comes from an Asian tree. It has a warm, aromatic, slightly bitter aniseed flavour and is available whole or ground. It is popular in Chinese cooking, and is used in marinades, stir-fries, bakes, cakes and some drinks. It goes particularly well with pork, poultry and fish as well as fruit.

CARAWAY

These seeds have a nutty, aniseed flavour and can be bought whole or ground. They are popular in German and Austrian cookery.

JUNIPER

These berries are available dried and are usually crushed to release their pungent pine flavour. Use them to flavour various meats.

CAYENNE PEPPER

This type of pepper is made from tropical chillies and it has a hot, spicy flavour. Use it to add a kick to South American and Caribbean dishes. It is especially good with seafood and chutneys.

PEPPERCORNS

The dried berries from the pepper plant come in black, white and green. Black peppercorns are the most widely used, and are available whole, cracked or ground. They deteriorate quickly when ground, so it is best to buy them whole and grind them yourself. They have an aromatic flavour and can be used in almost every savoury recipe and some sweet fruit dishes, such as balsamic strawberries.

CINNAMON

This spice comes from the bark of a tropical tree. The bark is dried and curled into quills or sticks; it can also be bought ground. Cinnamon has a sweet, aromatic smell and flavour, and is popular in Middle Eastern dishes. It is used to flavour a wide range of savoury and sweet dishes, such as stews, curries, pies, bread and cakes, and a whole host of desserts and drinks.

NUTMEG

Nutmeg has a sweet, fragrant flavour and is available whole or ground. It is used in a wide variety of savoury and sweet dishes, from meat, poultry, vegetables, beans, rice, cheese and eggs to chocolate, fruit, cream sauces and drinks.

CORIANDER

The dried seeds of the coriander plant are fragrant and lemony and can be used whole or ground. They are popular in marinades, chutneys, curries and bakes, and go particularly well with meat, poultry, fish, cheese, vegetables, beans, chocolate and jam.

CLOVES

These come from the buds of the tropical clove tree. The dried brown buds are sold whole or powdered, and have a sweet, pungent flavour. Push whole cloves into ham, pork, onions and oranges to flavour them, or use them ground in soups, stews, bread, cakes, desserts and chutneys. You can also use them whole in drinks such as mulled wine (but you should always remove whole cloves before serving).

MIXED SPICE

This blend of spices usually consists of allspice, cinnamon, cloves, ginger, coriander and nutmeg. It has a warm, sweet flavour and is delicious in fruit desserts, bread, cakes, biscuits and drinks.

CUMIN

These dried seeds have a pungent, nutty flavour and are also available ground. Cumin is popular in Asian and Mexican cooking, and goes well with beef, pork, salmon, shellfish, beans, pasta, eggs, cheese and rice.

FIVE SPICE

Chinese five-spice powder is, as its name implies, a blend of five spices, usually cloves, cinnamon, fennel seeds, Szechuan peppercorns and star anise. It has a sweet, pungent flavour and is popular in Chinese and Vietnamese cooking. It is especially good in stir-fries.

CURRY POWDER

This powder contains a mixture of spices including cardamom, chillies, cloves, coriander, fenugreek and turmeric. It is available mild or hot, and is used in curries, cream sauces and chutneys. It also goes well with beef, chicken, turkey, seafood, root vegetables, rice, eggs and cheese.

TURMERIC

This spice comes from the root of a tropical plant and has a pungent, somewhat bitter flavour. The powdered variety has a bright orange-yellow colour, so is used to tint foods as well as to flavour them.

GINGER

Ginger is available fresh or dried. The fresh root has a warm, lemon flavour and can be used chopped or grated. It is especially useful in marinades, salads, soups, stews and stir-fries; it can also be preserved in syrup. Powdered ginger has a more pungent, spicy flavour and is particularly good with fruit, biscuits, jams and chutneys.

BAKING

There is nothing like the aroma of freshly-baked bread, pastry, cakes and biscuits to stimulate the appetite. Baking these items for yourself is very satisfying, and the mouth-watering aromas will prove to be an irresistible temptation for friends and family.

MAKING BREAD AT HOME

Making your own bread does not have to be difficult – anyone can make delicious loaves and rolls with the minimum of effort. The key to making perfect bread is to use the right ingredients at the right temperature. Always use strong bread flour rather than ordinary flour: bread flour has a higher gluten content than ordinary flour, which increases the elasticity of the dough. You can use any of the different kinds of yeast, but each has a different method for breadmaking. You will also need to use the correct quantities: 15 g/½ oz fresh yeast or 1 tbsp dried yeast is enough to make 750 g/1 lb 10 oz strong bread flour rise. When you add water, make sure it is tepid because if it is too hot it will kill the yeast.

KEY TECHNIQUES FOR MAKING DOUGH

Making the perfect dough can be straightforward, but it is important to follow a certain procedure to achieve good results every time.

KNOCKING BACK

This process is also known as 'punching down'. After letting the dough rise for the first time for about an hour, simply punch your fist into the risen dough so that it collapses and releases the air. Then turn the dough out on to a floured work surface (some of it may need scraping out) and knead it for about 1 minute until it has lost its cold feel and has an even temperature.

PROVING

This stage literally means proving that the yeast is still active. To do this, after knocking back the dough, divide and shape it as required. Cover and leave it to rise for a second (but shorter) time, until the dough has doubled in size.

FRESH YEAST

Crush this in a jug with a little warm water, then cover and leave it to stand until the surface starts to bubble.

DRIED YEAST

Sprinkle the dried yeast over a little warm water in a jug, then stir in a pinch of sugar. Cover and leave to stand until it froths.

EASY-BLEND DRIED YEAST

Mix this yeast straight into the flour before the warm water is added.

FLOUR

Keep flour fresh by storing it in an airtight container in a cool, dry place. White flours will keep for 6-8 months and wholemeal flours for up to 2 months.

CORNFLOUR

This powdery flour is made from corn kernels and is used for thickening sauces, soups and desserts. It is usually mixed with a small quantity of cold liquid to make a smooth paste before being added to hot dishes.

PLAIN FLOUR

This flour is used for thickening sauces as well as for making batters and pastry.

SELF-RAISING FLOUR

Plain flour that has had baking powder and salt added is known as self-raising flour. It is used for making cakes and biscuits.

STRONG BREAD FLOUR

This flour is used for making bread. It contains a high level of gluten, which helps to give the bread dough its elasticity. If you are using a wholemeal variety, keep it in an airtight container in the refrigerator.

MALTED BROWN FLOUR

This is a brown flour that has had malted wheat grains added for a distinctive nutty flavour.

WHOLEMEAL FLOUR

This flour has a stronger flavour than white flour and contains wheatgerm, which means it has a higher fibre, fat and nutrient content. Store in an airtight container in the refrigerator.

BAKING & STORING BREAD

The dough will keep, covered, in the refrigerator for up to a day before baking. To bake the bread, you will need a hot oven, so make sure you preheat it beforehand. Underbaked bread has a moist, doughlike consistency and flavour, so it is always better to overbake if necessary. To test if the bread is properly baked, remove it from the oven, turn it out of its tin, and use your knuckles to give it a sharp tap on the bottom. If it sounds hollow, the bread is done. It it does not, return it to the oven and bake for another 5 minutes or until the bread is properly baked. When it is done, remove from the oven and leave to cool on a wire rack. If you want a soft crust, cover the loaf with a clean tea towel while it is cooling. Freshly baked bread will keep, covered, for 2–3 days at room temperature, but no longer because it has no added preservatives. You can also keep it wrapped in the refrigerator for up to a week, or wrap it in a freezer bag and freeze it for up to a month.

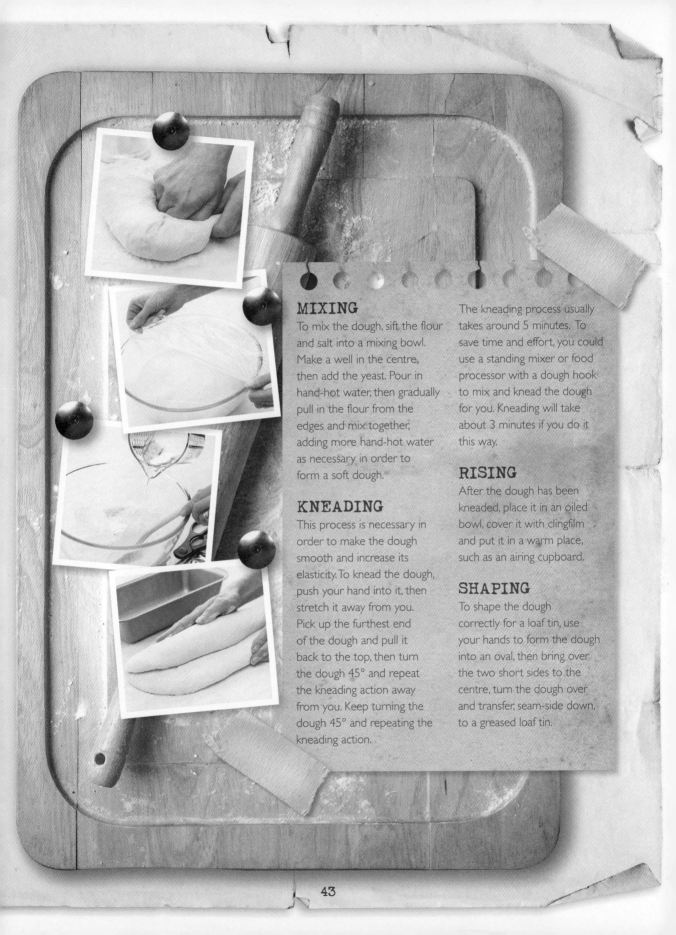

MIXING

To mix the dough, sift the flour and salt into a mixing bowl. Make a well in the centre, then add the yeast. Pour in hand-hot water, then gradually pull in the flour from the edges and mix together, adding more hand-hot water as necessary in order to form a soft dough.

KNEADING

This process is necessary in order to make the dough smooth and increase its elasticity. To knead the dough, push your hand into it, then stretch it away from you. Pick up the furthest end of the dough and pull it back to the top, then turn the dough 45° and repeat the kneading action away from you. Keep turning the dough 45° and repeating the kneading action.

The kneading process usually takes around 5 minutes. To save time and effort, you could use a standing mixer or food processor with a dough hook to mix and knead the dough for you. Kneading will take about 3 minutes if you do it this way.

RISING

After the dough has been kneaded, place it in an oiled bowl, cover it with clingfilm and put it in a warm place, such as an airing cupboard.

SHAPING

To shape the dough correctly for a loaf tin, use your hands to form the dough into an oval, then bring over the two short sides to the centre, turn the dough over and transfer, seam-side down, to a greased loaf tin.

CLASSIC RECIPES

Chicken Noodle Soup

SERVES 4–6

INGREDIENTS

- 2 skinless chicken breasts
- 1.2 litres/2 pints water or chicken stock
- 3 carrots, peeled and sliced into 5-mm/¼-inch slices
- 85 g/3 oz egg noodles
- salt and pepper
- fresh tarragon leaves, to garnish

1 Place the chicken breasts in a large saucepan over a medium heat, add the water and bring to a simmer. Cook for 25–30 minutes. Skim any foam from the surface if necessary. Remove the chicken from the stock and keep warm.

2 Continue to simmer the stock, add the carrots and noodles and cook for 4–5 minutes.

3 Thinly slice or shred the chicken breasts and place in warmed serving bowls.

4 Season the soup to taste with salt and pepper and pour over the chicken. Serve at once, garnished with the tarragon.

COOK'S TIP
Clean hands are the fastest tools for shredding cooked chicken, flaking cooked fish, crumbling cheese and tearing delicate salad leaves and herbs.

Split Pea & Ham Soup

SERVES 6–8

INGREDIENTS

- 500 g/1 lb 2 oz split green peas
- 1 tbsp olive oil
- 1 large onion, finely chopped
- 1 large carrot, finely chopped
- 1 celery stick, finely chopped
- 1 litre/1¾ pints chicken stock or vegetable stock
- 1 litre/1¾ pints water
- 225 g/8 oz lean smoked ham, finely diced
- ¼ tsp dried thyme
- ¼ tsp dried marjoram
- 1 bay leaf
- salt and pepper

1 Rinse the peas under cold running water. Put them in a saucepan and cover generously with water. Bring to the boil and boil for 3 minutes, skimming off the foam from the surface. Drain the peas.

2 Heat the oil in a large saucepan over a medium heat. Add the onion and cook for 3–4 minutes, stirring occasionally, until just softened.

3 Add the carrot and celery and continue cooking for 2 minutes. Add the peas, pour over the stock and water and stir to combine.

4 Bring just to the boil and stir the ham into the soup. Add the thyme, marjoram and bay leaf. Reduce the heat, cover and cook gently for 1–1½ hours, until the ingredients are very soft. Remove the bay leaf.

5 Taste and adjust the seasoning. Ladle into warmed soup bowls and serve.

Hints & Tips

_____

_____

_____

_____

_____

_____

_____

_____

_____

_____

_____

_____

_____

Recipe: _____
Serves: _____
Ingredients: _____
_____
_____
_____
_____
_____

Method:
_____
_____
_____
_____
_____
_____
_____
_____
_____
_____

Recipe: _____
Serves: _____
Ingredients: _____
_____
_____
_____
_____
_____

Method:
_____
_____
_____
_____
_____
_____
_____
_____
_____
_____

Just a Note...
_____
_____
_____
_____
_____
_____

Just a Note...
_____
_____
_____
_____
_____
_____

Hints & Tips

_____

_____

_____

_____

_____

_____

_____

_____

_____

_____

_____

_____

_____

_____

Recipe: _____
Serves: _____
Ingredients: _____
_____
_____
_____
_____

Method:
_____
_____
_____
_____
_____
_____
_____
_____
_____
_____

Recipe: _____
Serves: _____
Ingredients: _____
_____
_____
_____
_____

Method:
_____
_____
_____
_____
_____
_____
_____
_____
_____

Just a Note...

_____

_____

_____

_____

_____

_____

Just a Note...

_____

_____

_____

_____

_____

Hints & Tips

_____

_____

_____

_____

_____

_____

_____

_____

_____

_____

_____

_____

_____

_____

Recipe: _____
Serves: _____
Ingredients: _____
_____
_____
_____
_____

Method: _____
_____
_____
_____
_____
_____
_____
_____
_____
_____

Recipe: _____
Serves: _____
Ingredients: _____
_____
_____
_____
_____

Method: _____
_____
_____
_____
_____
_____
_____
_____
_____

Just a Note...
_____

_____

_____

_____

_____

_____

Just a Note...
_____

_____

_____

_____

_____

Barbecue-glazed Drumsticks

SERVES 6

INGREDIENTS

- 12 chicken drumsticks, about 1.6 kg/3 lb 8 oz
- 225 ml/8 fl oz barbecue sauce
- 1 tbsp soft light brown sugar
- 1 tbsp cider vinegar
- 1 tsp salt
- ½ tsp pepper
- ½ tsp Tabasco sauce
- vegetable oil, for brushing

1 Using a sharp knife, make 2 slashes, about 2.5 cm/1 inch apart, into the thickest part of the drumsticks, cutting to the bone. Put the drumsticks into a large, sealable polythene freezer bag.

2 Mix 4 tablespoons of the barbecue sauce, the sugar, vinegar, salt, pepper and Tabasco sauce together in a small bowl. Pour the mixture into the bag, press out most of the air and seal tightly. Shake the bag gently to distribute the sauce evenly and leave to marinate in the refrigerator for at least 4 hours.

3 Preheat the oven to 200°C/400°F/Gas Mark 6. Line a baking sheet with foil and brush lightly with oil.

4 Using tongs, transfer the drumsticks to the prepared baking sheet, spacing them evenly apart. Discard the marinade. Brush both sides of the drumsticks with some of the remaining barbecue sauce.

5 Bake for 15 minutes, then remove from the oven and brush generously with more barbecue sauce. Return to the oven and repeat this process three more times for a total cooking time of 1 hour. When done, the chicken will be cooked through with a thick, beautiful glaze.

CHILDREN'S FAVOURITE

Hints & Tips

Recipe: _____
Serves: _____
Ingredients: _____
_____
_____
_____
_____
_____

Method:
_____
_____
_____
_____
_____
_____
_____
_____
_____
_____

Recipe: _____
Serves: _____
Ingredients: _____
_____
_____
_____
_____
_____

Method:
_____
_____
_____
_____
_____
_____
_____
_____
_____
_____

Just a Note...
_____
_____
_____
_____
_____
_____

Just a Note...
_____
_____
_____
_____
_____
_____

Potato Pancakes

MAKES 12 PANCAKES

INGREDIENTS

- 4 large potatoes, peeled and coarsely grated
- 1 large onion, grated
- 2 eggs, lightly beaten
- 55 g/2 oz fine matzo meal
- 1 tsp salt
- pepper
- sunflower oil, for frying

TO SERVE
- soured cream
- thinly sliced smoked salmon
- snipped chives

1 Preheat the oven to 110°C/225°F/ Gas Mark ¼ and line a heatproof plate with kitchen paper. Working in small batches, put the potatoes on a tea towel, fold over the tea towel and squeeze to extract as much water as possible.

2 Put the potatoes in a large bowl, add the onion, eggs, matzo meal and the salt. Add the pepper to taste and mix together.

3 Heat a large, heavy-based frying pan over a medium–high heat. Add a thin layer of oil and heat until hot.

4 Drop 2 tablespoons of the batter into the pan and flatten slightly. Add as many more pancakes as will fit without overcrowding the pan. Fry for 2 minutes, or until crisp and golden underneath. Flip or turn with a palette knife and continue frying for a further 1–2 minutes, until crisp and golden.

5 Repeat this process using the remaining batter. Meanwhile, transfer the cooked pancakes to the prepared plate and keep warm in the preheated oven. Add extra oil to the pan between batches, if necessary.

6 Serve the pancakes hot, topped with soured cream and smoked salmon and sprinkled with chives.

IDEAL LIGHT BITE

Hints & Tips

_____

_____

_____

_____

_____

_____

_____

_____

_____

_____

_____

_____

_____

_____

Recipe: _____
Serves: _____
Ingredients: _____
_____
_____
_____
_____

Method: _____
_____
_____
_____
_____
_____
_____
_____
_____
_____

Recipe: _____
Serves: _____
Ingredients: _____
_____
_____
_____
_____

Method: _____
_____
_____
_____
_____
_____
_____
_____
_____
_____

Just a Note...

_____

_____

_____

_____

_____

Just a Note...

_____

_____

_____

_____

_____

Hints & Tips

Recipe: _____
Serves: _____
Ingredients: _____
_____
_____
_____
_____

Method:
_____
_____
_____
_____
_____
_____
_____
_____
_____

Recipe: _____
Serves: _____
Ingredients: _____
_____
_____
_____
_____

Method:
_____
_____
_____
_____
_____
_____
_____
_____
_____

Just a Note...

_____
_____
_____
_____
_____

Just a Note...

_____
_____
_____
_____
_____

Hints & Tips

_____

_____

_____

_____

_____

_____

_____

_____

_____

_____

_____

_____

_____

Recipe: _____
Serves: _____
Ingredients: _____
_____
_____
_____
_____

Method: _____
_____
_____
_____
_____
_____
_____
_____
_____

Recipe: _____
Serves: _____
Ingredients: _____
_____
_____
_____
_____

Method: _____
_____
_____
_____
_____
_____
_____
_____
_____

Just a Note...
_____
_____
_____
_____
_____
_____

Just a Note...
_____
_____
_____
_____
_____
_____

Mini Yorkshire Puddings

MAKES 6 PUDDINGS

INGREDIENTS

- 30 g/1 oz beef dripping or 2 tbsp sunflower oil
- 140 g/5 oz plain flour
- ½ tsp salt
- 2 eggs
- 225 ml/8 fl oz milk

1 Grease six metal pudding moulds with the dripping, then divide the remaining dripping between the moulds. Preheat the oven to 220°C/425°F/ Gas Mark 7, placing the moulds in the oven so the dripping can melt while the oven heats.

2 Sift together the flour and salt into a large mixing bowl and make a well in the centre. Break the eggs into the well, add the milk and beat, gradually drawing in the flour from the side to make a smooth batter. Remove the moulds from the oven and spoon in the batter until they are about half full.

3 Bake in the preheated oven for 30–35 minutes, without opening the door, until the puddings are well risen, puffed and golden brown. Serve immediately, as they will collapse if left to stand.

COOK'S TIP
Provide each child with a money box to start a savings habit. Let them keep whatever they find on regular coin hunts down the back of the sofa and under furniture.

Hints & Tips

Recipe: _____
Serves: _____
Ingredients: _____
_____
_____
_____
_____
_____

Method: _____
_____
_____
_____
_____
_____
_____
_____
_____
_____

Recipe: _____
Serves: _____
Ingredients: _____
_____
_____
_____
_____
_____

Method: _____
_____
_____
_____
_____
_____
_____
_____
_____
_____

Just a Note...
_____

_____

_____

_____

_____

Just a Note...
_____

_____

_____

_____

_____

Hints & Tips

_____

_____

_____

_____

_____

_____

_____

_____

_____

_____

_____

_____

_____

_____

Recipe: _____
Serves: _____
Ingredients: _____
_____
_____
_____
_____

Method: _____
_____
_____
_____
_____
_____
_____
_____
_____

Recipe: _____
Serves: _____
Ingredients: _____
_____
_____
_____
_____

Method: _____
_____
_____
_____
_____
_____
_____
_____

Just a Note...

_____

_____

_____

_____

_____

Just a Note...

_____

_____

_____

_____

_____

Hints & Tips

_____

_____

_____

_____

_____

_____

_____

_____

_____

_____

_____

_____

_____

_____

Recipe: _____
Serves: _____
Ingredients: _____
_____
_____
_____
_____

Method: _____
_____
_____
_____
_____
_____
_____
_____
_____

Recipe: _____
Serves: _____
Ingredients: _____
_____
_____
_____
_____

Method: _____
_____
_____
_____
_____
_____
_____

Just a Note...
_____
_____
_____
_____
_____

Just a Note...
_____
_____
_____
_____
_____

Roast Potatoes

SERVES 6

INGREDIENTS

- 1.3 kg/3 lb large floury potatoes, such as King Edward, Maris Piper or Desirée, peeled and cut into even-sized chunks
- 3 tbsp dripping, goose fat, duck fat or olive oil
- salt

1 Preheat the oven to 220°C/425°F/ Gas Mark 7.

2 Bring a large saucepan of lightly salted water to the boil, add the potatoes, bring back to the boil and cook for 5–7 minutes. The potatoes should still be firm. Remove from the heat.

3 Meanwhile, add the dripping to a roasting tin and place the tin in the preheated oven.

4 Drain the potatoes well and return them to the pan. Cover with the lid and firmly shake the pan so that the surface of the potatoes is roughened to help give a much crisper texture.

5 Remove the roasting tin from the oven and carefully tip the potatoes into the hot fat. Baste them to ensure they are all coated with the oil.

6 Roast at the top of the oven for 45–50 minutes until they are browned all over and thoroughly crisp. Turn the potatoes and baste again only once during the process or the crunchy edges will be destroyed.

7 Carefully transfer the potatoes from the roasting tin into a warmed serving dish. Sprinkle with a little salt and serve immediately.

GUILTY PLEASURE

Hints & Tips

_____
_____
_____
_____
_____
_____
_____
_____
_____
_____
_____
_____
_____

Recipe: _____
Serves: _____
Ingredients: _____
_____
_____
_____
_____

Method: _____
_____
_____
_____
_____
_____
_____

Recipe: _____
Serves: _____
Ingredients: _____
_____
_____
_____
_____

Method: _____
_____
_____
_____
_____
_____
_____

Just a Note...

_____
_____
_____
_____
_____

Just a Note...

_____
_____
_____
_____
_____

Hints & Tips

Recipe: _____
Serves: _____
Ingredients: _____
_____
_____
_____
_____
_____

Method: _____
_____
_____
_____
_____
_____
_____
_____
_____

Recipe: _____
Serves: _____
Ingredients: _____
_____
_____
_____
_____
_____

Method: _____
_____
_____
_____
_____
_____
_____
_____

Just a Note...

_____

_____

_____

_____

_____

_____

Just a Note...

_____

_____

_____

_____

_____

_____

FAMILY DINNERS

Roast Chicken

SERVES 6

INGREDIENTS

- 2.25 kg/5 lb free-range chicken
- 55 g/2 oz butter
- 2 tbsp chopped fresh lemon thyme
- 1 lemon, quartered
- 125 ml/4 fl oz white wine
- salt and pepper

1 Preheat the oven to 220°C/425°F/Gas Mark 7.

2 Make sure the chicken is clean, wiping it inside and out with kitchen paper, then place it in a roasting tin.

3 In a bowl, soften the butter with a fork, mix in the thyme and season well with salt and pepper.

4 Butter the chicken all over with the herb butter, inside and out, and place the lemon pieces inside the body cavity. Pour the wine over the chicken.

5 Roast in the centre of the preheated oven for 20 minutes. Reduce the temperature to 190°C/375°F/Gas Mark 5 and continue to roast for a further 1¼ hours, basting frequently. Cover with foil if the skin begins to brown too much. If the liquid in the tin dries out, add a little more wine or water.

6 Test that the chicken is cooked by piercing the thickest part of the leg with a sharp knife or skewer. If the juices run clear, the bird is done. Remove from the oven.

7 Place the chicken on a warmed serving plate, cover with foil and leave to rest for 10 minutes before carving.

8 Place the roasting tin on the hob and bubble the pan juices gently over a low heat, until they have reduced and are thick and glossy. Season to taste with salt and pepper.

9 Serve the chicken with the pan juices.

COOK'S TIP
To give more depth and a touch of sweetness to the finished dish, add a generous splash of Marsala to the pan juices when reducing them.

Hints & Tips

_____

_____

_____

_____

_____

_____

_____

_____

_____

_____

_____

_____

_____

_____

Recipe: _____
Serves: _____
Ingredients: _____
_____
_____
_____
_____

Method:
            _____
_____
_____
_____
_____
_____
_____
_____
_____

Recipe: _____
Serves: _____
Ingredients: _____
_____
_____
_____
_____

Method:
            _____
_____
_____
_____
_____
_____
_____
_____

Just a Note...
_____

_____

_____

_____

_____

_____

Just a Note...
_____

_____

_____

_____

_____

Hints & Tips

_____

_____

_____

_____

_____

_____

_____

_____

_____

_____

_____

_____

_____

Recipe: _____
Serves: _____
Ingredients: _____
_____
_____
_____
_____

Method: _____
_____
_____
_____
_____
_____
_____
_____
_____

Recipe: _____
Serves: _____
Ingredients: _____
_____
_____
_____
_____

Method: _____
_____
_____
_____
_____
_____
_____
_____
_____

Just a Note...
_____
_____
_____
_____
_____
_____

Just a Note...
_____
_____
_____
_____
_____
_____

Hints & Tips

_____

_____

_____

_____

_____

_____

_____

_____

_____

_____

_____

_____

_____

Recipe: _____
Serves: _____
Ingredients: _____
_____
_____
_____
_____

Method:
_____
_____
_____
_____
_____
_____
_____
_____
_____
_____

Recipe: _____
Serves: _____
Ingredients: _____
_____
_____
_____
_____

Method:
_____
_____
_____
_____
_____
_____
_____
_____
_____
_____

Just a Note...

_____

_____

_____

_____

_____

_____

Just a Note...

_____

_____

_____

_____

_____

_____

Hints & Tips

_____

_____

_____

_____

_____

_____

_____

_____

_____

_____

_____

_____

_____

_____

_____

Recipe: _____
Serves: _____
Ingredients: _____
_____
_____
_____
_____

Method: _____
_____
_____
_____
_____
_____
_____
_____
_____
_____

Recipe: _____
Serves: _____
Ingredients: _____
_____
_____
_____
_____

Method: _____
_____
_____
_____
_____
_____
_____
_____
_____
_____

Just a Note...
_____
_____
_____
_____
_____
_____

Just a Note...
_____
_____
_____
_____
_____
_____

Whole Roast Rib of Beef

SERVES 8
INGREDIENTS

- olive oil, for rubbing
- 3-kg/6 lb 8-oz joint of well-hung rib of beef on the bone
- ½ tbsp plain flour
- 200 ml/7 fl oz strong beef stock
- 200 ml/7 fl oz red wine
- salt and pepper

YORKSHIRE PUDDING
- 250 g/9 oz plain flour, sifted
- 6 eggs
- ½ tsp salt
- 600 ml/1 pint milk
- 2 tbsp vegetable oil or lard

ROAST POTATOES
- 2 kg/4 lb 8 oz roasting potatoes, peeled
- 6 tbsp sunflower oil, goose fat or duck fat
- salt and pepper

TO SERVE
- glazed carrots
- steamed broccoli
- horseradish sauce
- mustard

1 For the Yorkshire pudding, mix the flour, eggs and salt together in a bowl, then gradually add the milk as you stir with a whisk. When smooth set aside but do not chill.

2 For the roast potatoes, bring a large saucepan of lightly salted water to the boil, add the potatoes, bring back to the boil and cook for 10 minutes. Drain the potatoes and toss them in oil and salt and pepper. Put them in a roasting tin in a single layer.

3 Preheat the oven to 220°C/425°F/ Gas Mark 7. Put a 40 x 25-cm/16 x 10-inch roasting tin in the bottom of the oven to warm for the Yorkshire pudding.

4 Rub a generous amount of olive oil and salt and pepper into the beef, then place it in a roasting tin. Transfer to the preheated oven and roast for 30 minutes.

5 Reduce the temperature to 160°C/325°F/Gas Mark 3. Transfer the potatoes to the oven and roast with the beef for 60 minutes. Remove the beef from the oven and increase the oven temperature to 220°C/425°F/Gas Mark 7. Cover the beef with foil and leave to rest for at least 30 minutes.

6 Remove the roasting tin from the bottom of the oven and add the vegtable oil. Put it back in the oven for 5 minutes, then remove it and add the Yorkshire pudding batter. Put it back in the hot oven for about 20 minutes.

7 Meanwhile, make the gravy. Remove the beef from its tin and stir the flour into the leftover juices, add the stock and wine, then simmer over a medium heat until reduced by about half.

8 Remove the Yorkshire pudding and the potatoes from the oven. Cut the rib bones off the meat and carve the beef. Serve with the potatoes, Yorkshire pudding, carrots, broccoli, horseradish sauce and mustard.

HEART WARMING FOOD

Hints & Tips

_____

_____

_____

_____

_____

_____

_____

_____

_____

_____

_____

_____

_____

Recipe: _____
Serves: _____
Ingredients: _____
_____
_____
_____
_____

Method: _____
_____
_____
_____
_____
_____
_____
_____
_____
_____

Recipe: _____
Serves: _____
Ingredients: _____
_____
_____
_____
_____

Method: _____
_____
_____
_____
_____
_____
_____
_____
_____
_____

Just a Note...
_____
_____
_____
_____
_____
_____

Just a Note...
_____
_____
_____
_____
_____
_____

Meatloaf

SERVES 6–8
INGREDIENTS

- 100 g/3½ oz carrots, diced
- 55 g/2 oz celery, diced
- 1 onion, diced
- 1 red pepper, deseeded and chopped
- 4 large white mushrooms, sliced
- 25 g/1 oz butter
- 1 tbsp olive oil, plus extra for brushing
- 3 garlic cloves, peeled
- 1 tsp dried thyme
- 2 tsp finely chopped rosemary
- 1 tsp Worcestershire sauce
- 4 tbsp tomato ketchup
- ½ tsp cayenne pepper
- 1.1 kg/2 lb 8 oz beef mince, chilled
- 2 tsp salt
- 1 tsp pepper
- 2 eggs, beaten
- 55 g/2 oz fresh breadcrumbs
- peas and mashed potato, to serve

GLAZE

- 2 tbsp brown sugar
- 2 tbsp tomato ketchup
- 1 tbsp Dijon mustard
- salt

1 Put the vegetables into a food processor and pulse until very finely chopped, scraping down the bowl several times with a spatula.

2 Melt the butter with the oil and garlic in a large frying pan. Add the vegetable mixture and cook over a medium heat, stirring frequently, for about 10 minutes, until most of the moisture has evaporated and the mixture is lightly caramelized.

3 Remove the pan from the heat and stir in the thyme, rosemary, Worcestershire sauce, tomato ketchup and cayenne pepper. Leave to cool to room temperature.

4 Preheat the oven to 160°C/325°F/Gas Mark 3. Lightly brush a shallow roasting tin with olive oil.

5 Put the beef into a large bowl and gently break it up with your fingertips. Add the cooled vegetable mixture, salt, pepper and eggs and mix gently with your fingers for just 30 seconds. Add the breadcrumbs and continue to mix until combined. The less you work the meat, the better the texture of the meatloaf.

6 Put the meatloaf mixture in the centre of the prepared roasting tin, dampen your hands with cold water and shape it into a loaf about 15 cm/6 inches wide by 10 cm/4 inches high.

Dampen your hands again and smooth the surface. Bake in the centre of the preheated oven for 30 minutes.

7 Meanwhile, make the glaze. Whisk together the brown sugar, ketchup, Dijon mustard and a pinch of salt in a small bowl.

8 Remove the meatloaf from the oven and spread the glaze evenly over the top with a spoon and spread some down the sides as well. Return it to the oven and bake for a further 35–45 minutes, or until the internal temperature reaches 70°C/155°F on a meat thermometer. Remove and leave to rest for at least 15 minutes. Serve with peas and mashed potato.

Hints & Tips

_____

_____

_____

_____

_____

_____

_____

_____

_____

_____

_____

_____

_____

_____

Recipe: _____
Serves: _____
Ingredients: _____
_____
_____
_____
_____

Method: _____
_____
_____
_____
_____
_____
_____
_____
_____

Recipe: _____
Serves: _____
Ingredients: _____
_____
_____
_____
_____

Method: _____
_____
_____
_____
_____
_____
_____
_____

Just a Note...

_____
_____
_____
_____
_____

Just a Note...

_____
_____
_____
_____
_____

Poached Salmon

SERVES 6
INGREDIENTS

- 1 whole salmon (head on), about 2.7 kg/6 lb to 3.6 kg/ 8 lb prepared weight
- 3 tbsp salt
- 3 bay leaves
- 10 black peppercorns
- 1 onion, peeled and sliced
- 1 lemon, sliced
- lemon wedges, to serve

1 Wipe the salmon thoroughly inside and out with kitchen paper, then use the back of a cook's knife to remove any scales that might still be on the skin. Remove the fins with a pair of scissors and trim the tail. Some people prefer to cut off the head but it is traditionally served with it on.

2 Place the salmon on the two-handled rack that comes with a fish kettle, then place it in the kettle. Fill the kettle with enough cold water to cover the salmon adequately. Sprinkle over the salt, bay leaves and peppercorns and scatter in the onion and lemon slices.

3 Place the kettle over a low heat, over two burners, and very slowly bring just to the boil.

4 Cover and simmer very gently. To serve cold, simmer for 2 minutes only, remove from the heat and leave to cool in the water for about 2 hours with the lid on. To serve hot, simmer for 6–8 minutes and leave to stand in the hot water for 15 minutes before removing. Serve with lemon wedges for squeezing over.

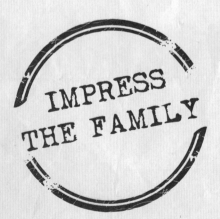

IMPRESS THE FAMILY

Hints & Tips

_____
_____
_____
_____
_____
_____
_____
_____
_____
_____
_____
_____

Recipe: _____
Serves: _____
Ingredients: _____
_____
_____
_____
_____

Method: _____
_____
_____
_____
_____
_____
_____
_____
_____

Recipe: _____
Serves: _____
Ingredients: _____
_____
_____
_____
_____

Method: _____
_____
_____
_____
_____
_____
_____
_____
_____

Just a Note...
_____

_____

_____

_____

_____

Just a Note...
_____

_____

_____

_____

_____

Hints & Tips

_____

_____

_____

_____

_____

_____

_____

_____

_____

_____

_____

_____

_____

Recipe: _____
Serves: _____
Ingredients: _____
_____
_____
_____
_____

Method:
            _____
_____
_____
_____
_____
_____
_____
_____
_____
_____
_____

Recipe: _____
Serves: _____
Ingredients: _____
_____
_____
_____
_____

Method:
            _____
_____
_____
_____
_____
_____
_____
_____
_____
_____

Just a Note...

_____

_____

_____

_____

_____

_____

Just a Note...

_____

_____

_____

_____

_____

_____

Hints & Tips

_____

_____

_____

_____

_____

_____

_____

_____

_____

_____

_____

_____

_____

Recipe: _____
Serves: _____
Ingredients: _____
_____
_____
_____
_____

Method: _____
_____
_____
_____
_____
_____
_____
_____

Recipe: _____
Serves: _____
Ingredients: _____
_____
_____
_____
_____

Method: _____
_____
_____
_____
_____
_____
_____
_____

Just a Note...
_____
_____
_____
_____
_____
_____

Just a Note...
_____
_____
_____
_____
_____
_____

Asparagus & Tomato Tart

SERVES 4

INGREDIENTS

- butter, for greasing
- 375 g/13 oz ready-made shortcrust pastry, thawed, if frozen
- 1 bunch thin asparagus spears
- 250 g/9 oz spinach leaves
- 3 large eggs, beaten
- 150 ml/5 fl oz double cream
- 1 garlic clove, crushed
- 10 small cherry tomatoes, halved
- handful fresh basil, chopped
- 25 g/1 oz grated Parmesan cheese
- salt and pepper

1 Preheat the oven to 190°C/375°F/ Gas Mark 5. Grease a 25–30-cm/10–12-inch tart tin with butter, then roll out the pastry and use to line the prepared tin.

2 Cut off any excess pastry, prick the base with a fork, cover with a piece of greaseproof paper and fill with baking beans, then bake blind in the preheated oven for 20–30 minutes until lightly browned. Remove from the oven and leave to cool slightly. Reduce the oven temperature to 180°C/350°F/Gas Mark 4.

3 Meanwhile, bend the asparagus spears until they snap, and discard the woody ends. Bring a large saucepan of lightly salted water to the boil, add the asparagus and blanch for 1 minute, then remove and drain. Add the spinach to the boiling water, then remove immediately and drain very well.

4 Mix the eggs, cream and garlic together and season to taste with salt and pepper. Lay the blanched spinach at the bottom of the pastry base, add the asparagus and tomatoes, cut side up, in any arrangement you like, scatter over the basil, and pour the egg mixture on top.

5 Transfer to the oven and bake for about 35 minutes, or until the filling has set. Sprinkle the cheese on top and leave to cool to room temperature before serving.

COOK'S TIP
This is a great dish to make for summer picnics and garden parties. The ingredients are interchangeable with other crisp spring and summer vegetables.

Hints & Tips

Recipe: _____
Serves: _____
Ingredients: _____
_____
_____
_____
_____

Method:
_____
_____
_____
_____
_____
_____
_____
_____
_____
_____

Recipe: _____
Serves: _____
Ingredients: _____
_____
_____
_____
_____

Method:
_____
_____
_____
_____
_____
_____
_____
_____
_____
_____

Just a Note...

_____
_____
_____
_____
_____
_____

Just a Note...

_____
_____
_____
_____
_____

Hints & Tips

_____

_____

_____

_____

_____

_____

_____

_____

_____

_____

_____

_____

_____

Recipe: _____
Serves: _____
Ingredients: _____
_____
_____
_____
_____

Method:
_____ _____
_____
_____
_____
_____
_____
_____
_____

Recipe: _____
Serves: _____
Ingredients: _____
_____
_____
_____
_____

Method:
_____ _____
_____
_____
_____
_____
_____
_____
_____

Just a Note...
_____

_____

_____

_____

_____

Just a Note...
_____

_____

_____

_____

_____

Hints & Tips

Recipe: _____
Serves: _____
Ingredients: _____
_____
_____
_____
_____
_____

Method: _____
_____
_____
_____
_____
_____
_____
_____
_____
_____

Recipe: _____
Serves: _____
Ingredients: _____
_____
_____
_____
_____
_____

Method: _____
_____
_____
_____
_____
_____
_____
_____
_____

Just a Note...
_____

_____

_____

_____

_____

_____

Just a Note...
_____

_____

_____

_____

_____

_____

BAKING DAY

Victoria Sponge Cake

SERVES 8–10

INGREDIENTS

- 175 g/6 oz butter, at room temperature, plus extra for greasing
- 175 g/6 oz caster sugar
- 3 eggs, beaten
- 175 g/6 oz self-raising flour
- pinch of salt
- 3 tbsp raspberry jam
- 1 tbsp caster sugar or icing sugar, for sprinkling

1 Preheat the oven to 180°C/350°F/Gas Mark 4.

2 Grease two 20-cm/8-inch sponge tins and line with greaseproof paper or baking paper.

3 Cream the butter and sugar together in a mixing bowl using a wooden spoon or a hand-held mixer until the mixture is pale in colour and light and fluffy.

4 Add the eggs a little at a time, beating well after each addition.

5 Sift the flour and salt together and carefully add to the mixture, folding in with a metal spoon or a spatula. Divide the mixture between the tins and smooth over with the spatula.

6 Place them on the same shelf in the centre of the preheated oven and bake for 25–30 minutes until well risen, golden brown and beginning to shrink from the sides of the tins.

7 Remove from the oven and leave to stand in the tins for 1 minute.

8 Loosen the cakes from around the edges of the tins using a palette knife. Turn the cakes out onto a clean tea towel, remove the paper and invert them onto a wire rack (this prevents the wire rack marking the tops of the cakes).

9 When completely cool, sandwich together with the jam and sprinkle with the sugar. The cake is delicious when freshly baked, but any remaining cake can be stored in an airtight tin for up to 1 week.

FEEL-BETTER FOOD

Hints & Tips

_____

_____

_____

_____

_____

_____

_____

_____

_____

_____

_____

_____

_____

_____

_____

Recipe: _____
Serves: _____
Ingredients: _____
_____
_____
_____
_____

Method: _____
_____
_____
_____
_____
_____
_____
_____
_____
_____

Recipe: _____
Serves: _____
Ingredients: _____
_____
_____
_____
_____

Method: _____
_____
_____
_____
_____
_____
_____
_____
_____
_____

Just a Note...

_____
_____
_____
_____
_____
_____

Just a Note...

_____
_____
_____
_____
_____
_____

Apple Pie

SERVES 6

INGREDIENTS

PASTRY
- 350 g/12 oz plain flour
- pinch of salt
- 85 g/3 oz butter or margarine, cut into small pieces
- 85 g/3 oz lard or white vegetable fat, cut into small pieces
- about 6 tbsp cold water
- beaten egg or milk, for glazing

FILLING
- 750 g–1 kg/1 lb 10 oz– 2 lb 4 oz cooking apples, peeled, cored and sliced
- 125 g/4½ oz soft light brown sugar or caster sugar, plus extra for sprinkling
- ½–1 tsp ground cinnamon, mixed spice or ground ginger
- 1–2 tbsp water (optional)

1 To make the pastry, sift together the flour and salt into a mixing bowl. Add the butter and lard and rub in with your fingertips until the mixture resembles fine breadcrumbs. Add the water and gather the mixture together into a dough. Wrap the dough in clingfilm and chill it in the refrigerator for 30 minutes.

2 Preheat the oven to 220°C/425°F/ Gas Mark 7. Roll out almost two thirds of the pastry thinly and use it to line a deep 23-cm/9-inch pie plate or pie tin.

3 To make the filling, mix the apples with the sugar and cinnamon and pack into the pastry case. Add the water if needed, particularly if the apples are not very juicy.

4 Roll out the remaining pastry to form a lid. Dampen the edges of the pie rim with water and position the lid, pressing the edges firmly together. Trim and crimp the edges.

5 Using the trimmings, cut out leaves or other shapes to decorate the top of the pie. Dampen and attach. Glaze the top of the pie with beaten egg and make one or two slits in the top.

6 Place the pie on a baking tray and bake in the preheated oven for 20 minutes, then reduce the oven temperature to 180°C/350°F/Gas Mark 4 and bake for a further 30 minutes, or until the pastry is a light golden brown. Serve hot or cold, sprinkled with sugar.

COOK'S TIP
Prevent apples discoloring by placing the peeled slices in a bowl of water with the juice of 1 lemon added.

Hints & Tips

_____

_____

_____

_____

_____

_____

_____

_____

_____

_____

_____

_____

_____

_____

Recipe: _____

Serves: _____

Ingredients: _____

_____

_____

_____

_____

Method:
_____

_____

_____

_____

_____

_____

_____

_____

_____

Recipe: _____

Serves: _____

Ingredients: _____

_____

_____

_____

_____

Method:
_____

_____

_____

_____

_____

_____

_____

_____

_____

Just a Note...

_____

_____

_____

_____

_____

_____

Just a Note...

_____

_____

_____

_____

_____

_____

Hints & Tips

_____
_____
_____
_____
_____
_____
_____
_____
_____
_____
_____
_____
_____
_____
_____

Recipe: _____
Serves: _____
Ingredients: _____
_____
_____
_____
_____
_____

Method:
_____
_____
_____
_____
_____
_____
_____
_____

Recipe: _____
Serves: _____
Ingredients: _____
_____
_____
_____
_____
_____

Method:
_____
_____
_____
_____
_____
_____
_____
_____

Just a Note...
_____
_____
_____
_____
_____

Just a Note...
_____
_____
_____
_____
_____

Hints & Tips

Recipe: _____
Serves: _____
Ingredients: _____
_____
_____
_____
_____

Method: _____
_____
_____
_____
_____
_____
_____
_____
_____

Recipe: _____
Serves: _____
Ingredients: _____
_____
_____
_____
_____

Method: _____
_____
_____
_____
_____
_____
_____
_____
_____

Just a Note...

_____

_____

_____

_____

_____

_____

Just a Note...

_____

_____

_____

_____

_____

_____

Blueberry Crumb Cake

SERVES 12
INGREDIENTS

- 280 g/10 oz fresh blueberries
- 450 g/1 lb self-raising flour, plus extra for dusting
- 1¼ tsp salt
- ½ tsp mixed spice
- 280 g/10 oz butter, at room temperature, plus extra for greasing
- 350 g/12 oz caster sugar
- ½ tsp vanilla extract
- ½ tsp almond extract
- 2 large eggs
- 300–350 ml/10–12 fl oz soured cream

CRUMB TOPPING

- 115 g/4 oz butter, diced
- 140 g/5 oz plain flour
- 2 tbsp soft light brown sugar
- 1 tbsp granulated sugar
- 85 g/3 oz almonds, chopped

1 For the crumb topping, put the butter and flour into a large bowl and rub together until the mixture resembles coarse breadcrumbs. Stir in both types of sugar and the almonds, then leave to chill in the refrigerator until required.

2 Preheat the oven to 180°C/350°F/Gas Mark 4. Grease a 33 × 23-cm/ 13 × 9-inch rectangular cake tin and line with baking paper. Dust the blueberries with 1 tablespoon of the measured flour and set aside. Sift the remaining flour into a bowl with the salt and mixed spice and set aside.

3 Place the butter in a large bowl and, using an electric mixer, beat until soft and creamy. Add the sugar, vanilla extract and almond extract and continue beating

until the mixture is light and fluffy. Add the eggs, one at a time, beating well after each addition, then beat in 300 ml/10 fl oz of the soured cream. Beat in the flour until the mixture is soft and falls easily from a spoon. Add the remaining soured cream, 1 tablespoon at a time, if necessary.

4 Add the blueberries and any loose flour to the batter and quickly fold in. Pour the batter into the prepared tin and smooth the surface. Pinch the topping into large crumbs and scatter evenly over the batter.

5 Bake the cake in the preheated oven for 45–55 minutes until it comes away from the side of the tin and a cocktail stick inserted into the centre comes out clean. Transfer the tin to a wire rack and leave it to cool completely. Cut the cake into 12 slices and serve straight from the tin.

COOK'S TIP
When a recipe says 'dot with butter', shave off curls from a cold block with a vegetable peeler.

Hints & Tips

_____

_____

_____

_____

_____

_____

_____

_____

_____

_____

_____

_____

_____

Recipe: _____
Serves: _____
Ingredients: _____
_____
_____
_____
_____
_____

Method:
_____
_____
_____
_____
_____
_____
_____
_____
_____
_____
_____

Recipe: _____
Serves: _____
Ingredients: _____
_____
_____
_____
_____
_____

Method:
_____
_____
_____
_____
_____
_____
_____
_____
_____
_____
_____

Just a Note...
_____
_____
_____
_____
_____

Just a Note...
_____
_____
_____
_____
_____

Mega Chip Cookies

MAKES 12 LARGE COOKIES
INGREDIENTS

- 225 g/8 oz butter, softened
- 140 g/5 oz caster sugar
- 1 egg yolk, lightly beaten
- 2 tsp vanilla extract
- 225 g/8 oz plain flour
- 55 g/2 oz cocoa powder
- pinch of salt
- 85 g/3 oz milk chocolate chips
- 85 g/3 oz white chocolate chips
- 115 g/4 oz plain chocolate, coarsely chopped

1 Preheat the oven to 190°C/375°F/Gas Mark 5. Line 2–3 baking sheets with baking parchment.

2 Put the butter and sugar into a bowl and mix well with a wooden spoon, then beat in the egg yolk and vanilla extract. Sift together the flour, cocoa powder and salt into the mixture, then add the milk chocolate chips and white chocolate chips and stir until thoroughly combined.

3 Make 12 balls of the mixture, place them on the prepared baking sheets, spaced well apart, and flatten slightly. Press the pieces of plain chocolate into the cookies.

4 Bake in the preheated oven for 12–15 minutes. Leave to cool on the baking sheets for 5–10 minutes, then, using a palette knife, carefully transfer the cookies to wire racks to cool completely.

CHILDREN'S FAVOURITE

Cinnamon Swirls

MAKES 12 SWIRLS

INGREDIENTS

- 225 g/8 oz strong white flour
- ½ tsp salt
- 7 g/¼ oz easy-blend dried yeast
- 2 tbsp butter, cut into small pieces, plus extra for greasing
- 1 egg, lightly beaten
- 125 ml/4 fl oz lukewarm milk
- 2 tbsp maple syrup, for glazing

FILLING
- 4 tbsp butter, softened
- 2 tsp ground cinnamon
- 50 g/1¾ oz soft light brown sugar
- 50 g/1¾ oz currants

1 Grease a baking sheet with a little butter.

2 Sift together the flour and salt into a mixing bowl. Stir in the yeast. Rub in the butter with your fingertips until the mixture resembles breadcrumbs. Add the egg and milk and mix to form a dough.

3 Form the dough into a ball, place in a greased bowl, cover and leave to stand in a warm place for about 40 minutes, or until doubled in size.

4 Lightly knock back the dough for 1 minute, then roll out to a rectangle measuring 30 x 23 cm/ 12 x 9 inches.

5 To make the filling, cream the butter, cinnamon and sugar together until light and fluffy. Spread the filling evenly over the dough rectangle, leaving a 2.5-cm/1-inch border all around. Sprinkle the currants evenly over the top.

6 Roll up the dough from one of the long edges, and press down to seal. Cut the roll into 12 slices. Place them, cut-side down, on the baking sheet, cover and leave to stand for 30 minutes.

7 Meanwhile, preheat the oven to 190°C/375°F/ Gas Mark 5. Bake the swirls in the preheated oven for 20–30 minutes, or until well risen. Brush with the maple syrup and leave to cool slightly before serving.

Hints & Tips

Recipe: _____
Serves: _____
Ingredients: _____
_____
_____
_____
_____

Method: _____
_____
_____
_____
_____
_____
_____
_____
_____

Recipe: _____
Serves: _____
Ingredients: _____
_____
_____
_____
_____

Method: _____
_____
_____
_____
_____
_____
_____
_____
_____

Just a Note...
_____
_____
_____
_____
_____

Just a Note...
_____
_____
_____
_____
_____

Hints & Tips

_____

_____

_____

_____

_____

_____

_____

_____

_____

_____

_____

_____

Recipe: _____
Serves: _____
Ingredients: _____
_____
_____
_____
_____

Method: _____
_____
_____
_____
_____
_____
_____
_____
_____

Recipe: _____
Serves: _____
Ingredients: _____
_____
_____
_____
_____

Method: _____
_____
_____
_____
_____
_____
_____
_____
_____

Just a Note...

_____

_____

_____

_____

_____

_____

Just a Note...

_____

_____

_____

_____

_____

_____

Hints & Tips

Recipe: _____
Serves: _____
Ingredients: _____
_____
_____
_____
_____

Method: _____
_____
_____
_____
_____
_____
_____
_____
_____

Recipe: _____
Serves: _____
Ingredients: _____
_____
_____
_____
_____

Method: _____
_____
_____
_____
_____
_____
_____
_____
_____

Just a Note...
_____
_____
_____
_____
_____

Just a Note...
_____
_____
_____
_____
_____

Hints & Tips

_____

_____

_____

_____

_____

_____

_____

_____

_____

_____

_____

_____

_____

Recipe: _____
Serves: _____
Ingredients: _____
_____
_____
_____
_____

Method:
_____
_____
_____
_____
_____
_____
_____
_____
_____
_____

Recipe: _____
Serves: _____
Ingredients: _____
_____
_____
_____
_____

Method:
_____
_____
_____
_____
_____
_____
_____
_____
_____
_____

Just a Note...
_____
_____
_____
_____
_____

Just a Note...
_____
_____
_____
_____
_____

Hints & Tips

_____

_____

_____

_____

_____

_____

_____

_____

_____

_____

_____

_____

_____

_____

Recipe: _____
Serves: _____
Ingredients: _____
_____
_____
_____

_____

Method: _____
_____
_____
_____
_____
_____
_____
_____

Recipe: _____
Serves: _____
Ingredients: _____
_____
_____
_____

_____

Method: _____
_____
_____
_____
_____
_____
_____
_____

Just a Note...

_____

_____

_____

_____

_____

Just a Note...

_____

_____

_____

_____

_____

Hints & Tips

_____

_____

_____

_____

_____

_____

_____

_____

_____

_____

_____

_____

Recipe: _____
Serves: _____
Ingredients: _____
_____
_____
_____
_____

Method: _____
_____
_____
_____
_____
_____
_____
_____
_____
_____

Recipe: _____
Serves: _____
Ingredients: _____
_____
_____
_____
_____

Method: _____
_____
_____
_____
_____
_____
_____
_____
_____
_____

Just a Note...
_____
_____
_____
_____
_____

Just a Note...
_____
_____
_____
_____
_____

Cornbread

MAKES I SMALL LOAF

INGREDIENTS

- vegetable oil, for greasing
- 175 g/6 oz plain flour
- 1 tsp salt
- 4 tsp baking powder
- 1 tsp caster sugar
- 280 g/10 oz polenta
- 115 g/4 oz butter, softened
- 4 eggs
- 250 ml/8 fl oz milk
- 3 tbsp double cream

1 Preheat the oven to 200°C/400°F/Gas Mark 6. Brush a 20-cm/8-inch square cake tin with oil.

2 Sift together the flour, salt and baking powder into a bowl. Add the sugar and polenta and stir to mix. Add the butter and cut into the dry ingredients with a knife, then rub it in with your fingertips until the mixture resembles fine breadcrumbs.

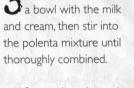

3 Lightly beat the eggs in a bowl with the milk and cream, then stir into the polenta mixture until thoroughly combined.

4 Spoon the mixture into the prepared tin and smooth the surface. Bake in the preheated oven for 30–35 minutes, until a wooden cocktail stick inserted into the centre of the loaf comes out clean. Remove the tin from the oven and leave to cool for 5–10 minutes, then cut into squares and serve warm.

PRACTICE MAKES PERFECT

Hints & Tips

_____

_____

_____

_____

_____

_____

_____

_____

_____

_____

_____

_____

_____

Recipe: _____
Serves: _____
Ingredients: _____
_____
_____
_____
_____
_____

Method: _____
_____
_____
_____
_____
_____
_____
_____
_____
_____
_____

Recipe: _____
Serves: _____
Ingredients: _____
_____
_____
_____
_____
_____

Method: _____
_____
_____
_____
_____
_____
_____
_____
_____
_____

Just a Note...
_____
_____
_____
_____
_____
_____
_____

Just a Note...
_____
_____
_____
_____
_____
_____
_____

DELICIOUS
DESSERTS

Rhubarb Crumble

SERVES 6

INGREDIENTS

- 900 g/2 lb rhubarb
- 115 g/4 oz caster sugar
- grated rind and juice of 1 orange
- custard or cream, to serve

CRUMBLE

- 225 g/8 oz plain flour or wholemeal flour
- 115 g/4 oz butter
- 115 g/4 oz soft light brown sugar
- 1 tsp ground ginger

1 Preheat the oven to 190°C/375°F/Gas Mark 5.

2 Cut the rhubarb into 2.5-cm/1-inch lengths and place in a 1.7-litre/3-pint ovenproof dish with the sugar and the orange rind and juice.

3 To make the crumble, place the flour in a mixing bowl and rub in the butter until the mixture resembles coarse breadcrumbs. Stir in the sugar and the ginger.

4 Spread the crumble evenly over the fruit and press down lightly using a fork.

5 Place on a baking tray and bake in the centre of the preheated oven for 25–30 minutes, until the crumble is golden brown. Serve warm with custard.

COOK'S TIP
Use very young shoots of rhubarb as they are the sweetest. A handful of strawberries would be a good addition as they enhance the flavour and colour.

Hints & Tips

Recipe: _____
Serves: _____
Ingredients: _____
_____
_____
_____
_____

Method: _____
_____
_____
_____
_____
_____
_____
_____
_____

Recipe: _____
Serves: _____
Ingredients: _____
_____
_____
_____
_____

Method: _____
_____
_____
_____
_____
_____
_____
_____

Just a Note...
_____
_____
_____
_____
_____

Just a Note...
_____
_____
_____
_____
_____

Hints & Tips

Recipe: _____
Serves: _____
Ingredients: _____
_____
_____
_____

Method:
            _____
_____
_____
_____
_____
_____
_____
_____
_____

Recipe: _____
Serves: _____
Ingredients: _____
_____
_____
_____

Method:
            _____
_____
_____
_____
_____
_____
_____
_____
_____

Just a Note...

_____

_____

_____

_____

_____

_____

Just a Note...

_____

_____

_____

_____

_____

_____

Hints & Tips

_____

_____

_____

_____

_____

_____

_____

_____

_____

_____

_____

_____

Recipe: _____

Serves: _____

Ingredients: _____

_____

_____

_____

_____

Method: _____

_____

_____

_____

_____

_____

_____

_____

_____

_____

Recipe: _____

Serves: _____

Ingredients: _____

_____

_____

_____

_____

Method: _____

_____

_____

_____

_____

_____

_____

_____

_____

_____

Just a Note...

_____

_____

_____

_____

_____

Just a Note...

_____

_____

_____

_____

_____

Hints & Tips

Recipe: _____
Serves: _____
Ingredients: _____
_____
_____
_____
_____
_____

Method: _____
_____
_____
_____
_____
_____
_____
_____
_____
_____

Recipe: _____
Serves: _____
Ingredients: _____
_____
_____
_____
_____
_____

Method: _____
_____
_____
_____
_____
_____
_____
_____
_____
_____

Just a Note...
_____
_____
_____
_____
_____
_____

Just a Note...
_____
_____
_____
_____
_____
_____

Banana Cream Pie

SERVES 8–10
INGREDIENTS

- flour, for dusting
- 350 g/12 oz ready-made shortcrust pastry, thawed, if frozen
- 4 large egg yolks
- 85 g/3 oz caster sugar
- 4 tbsp cornflour
- pinch of salt
- 450 ml/16 fl oz milk
- 1 tsp vanilla extract
- 3 bananas
- ½ tbsp lemon juice
- 350 ml/12 fl oz double cream, whipped with 3 tbsp icing sugar, to decorate

1 Preheat the oven to 200°C/400°F/ Gas Mark 6. Very lightly flour a rolling pin and use to roll out the pastry on a lightly floured work surface into a 30-cm/12-inch round. Line a 23-cm/9-inch pie plate with the pastry, then trim the excess pastry and prick the base all over with a fork. Line the pastry case with greaseproof paper and fill with baking beans.

2 Bake in the preheated oven for 15 minutes, or until the pastry is a light golden colour. Remove the paper and beans and prick the base again. Return to the oven and bake for a further 5–10 minutes, until golden and dry. Leave to cool completely on a wire rack.

3 Meanwhile, put the egg yolks, sugar, cornflour and salt into a bowl and beat until blended and pale in colour. Beat in the milk and vanilla extract.

4 Pour the mixture into a heavy-based saucepan over a medium–high heat and bring to the boil, stirring, until smooth and thick. Reduce the heat to low and simmer, stirring, for 2 minutes. Strain the mixture into a bowl and set aside to cool.

5 Slice the bananas, place in a bowl with the lemon juice and toss. Arrange them in the cooled pastry case, then top with the custard and chill in the refrigerator for at least 2 hours. Spread the cream over the top of the pie and serve immediately.

COOK'S TIP
Old-fashioned metal pie plates, cake tins and tart tins conduct heat better than glass, earthenware or porcelain, producing even baking and reducing the cooking time.

New York Cheesecake

SERVES 10

INGREDIENTS

- 100 g/3½ oz butter, plus extra for greasing
- 150 g/5½ oz digestive biscuits, finely crushed
- 1 tbsp granulated sugar
- 900 g/2 lb cream cheese
- 250 g/9 oz caster sugar
- 2 tbsp plain flour
- 1 tsp vanilla extract
- finely grated zest of 1 orange
- finely grated zest of 1 lemon
- 3 eggs
- 2 egg yolks
- 300 ml/10 fl oz double cream

1 Preheat the oven to 180°C/350°F/Gas Mark 4. Place a small saucepan over a low flame, add the butter and heat until it melts. Remove from the heat, stir in the biscuits and granulated sugar and mix thoroughly.

2 Press the biscuit mixture tightly into the base of a 23-cm/9-inch springform cake tin. Place in the preheated oven and bake for 10 minutes. Remove from the oven and leave it to cool on a wire rack.

3 Increase the oven temperature to 200°C/400°F/Gas Mark 6. Use an electric mixer to beat the cheese until creamy, then gradually add the caster sugar and flour and beat until smooth. Increase the speed and beat in the vanilla extract, orange zest and lemon zest, then beat in the eggs and egg yolks one at a time. Finally, beat in the cream. Scrape any excess from the sides and paddles of the beater into the mixture. It should be light and fluffy – beat on a faster setting if you need to.

4 Grease the side of the cake tin and pour in the filling. Smooth the top, transfer to the preheated oven and bake in the oven for 15 minutes, then reduce the temperature to 100°C/200°F/Gas Mark ¼ and bake for a further 30 minutes. Turn off the oven and leave the cheesecake in it for 2 hours to cool and set. Cover and chill in the refrigerator overnight.

5 Slide a knife around the edge of the cake then unfasten the tin, cut the cheesecake into slices and serve.

GUILTY PLEASURE

Hints & Tips

_____

_____

_____

_____

_____

_____

_____

_____

_____

_____

_____

_____

_____

Recipe: _____
Serves: _____
Ingredients: _____
_____
_____
_____
_____

Method: _____
_____
_____
_____
_____
_____
_____
_____
_____

Recipe: _____
Serves: _____
Ingredients: _____
_____
_____
_____
_____

Method: _____
_____
_____
_____
_____
_____
_____
_____

Just a Note...

_____
_____
_____
_____
_____

Just a Note...

_____
_____
_____
_____
_____

Hints & Tips

_____

_____

_____

_____

_____

_____

_____

_____

_____

_____

_____

_____

_____

_____

Recipe: _____
Serves: _____
Ingredients: _____
_____
_____
_____
_____
_____

Method:
              _____
_____
_____
_____
_____
_____
_____
_____
_____

Recipe: _____
Serves: _____
Ingredients: _____
_____
_____
_____
_____
_____

Method:
              _____
_____
_____
_____
_____
_____
_____
_____
_____

Just a Note...

_____

_____

_____

_____

_____

Just a Note...

_____

_____

_____

_____

_____

Bread & Butter Pudding

SERVES 4–6

INGREDIENTS

- 85 g/3 oz butter, softened
- 6 slices thick white bread
- 55 g/2 oz mixed dried fruit, such as sultanas, currants and raisins
- 25 g/1 oz mixed peel
- 3 large eggs
- 300 ml/10 fl oz milk
- 150 ml/5 fl oz double cream
- 55 g/2 oz caster sugar
- whole nutmeg, for grating
- 1 tbsp demerara sugar

1 Preheat the oven to 180°C/350°F/ Gas Mark 4.

2 Use a little of the butter to grease a 20 x 25-cm/ 8 x 10-inch baking dish. Butter the slices of bread, cut them into quarters and arrange half of the slices overlapping in the prepared baking dish.

3 Scatter half the fruit and mixed peel over the bread, cover with the remaining bread slices, then add the remaining fruit and mixed peel.

4 In a mixing jug, whisk the eggs well and mix in the milk, cream and caster sugar. Pour over the pudding and leave to stand for 15 minutes to allow the bread to soak up some of the egg mixture. Tuck in most of the fruit to prevent it burning.

5 Grate nutmeg to taste over the top of the pudding, then sprinkle over the demerara sugar.

6 Place the pudding on a baking tray and bake at the top of the preheated oven for 30–40 minutes, until just set and golden brown.

7 Remove from the oven and serve warm.

COOK'S TIP
Try using brioche or a lightly fruited loaf instead of white bread. Any mixture of dried fruits can be used. Why not experiment with your favourites?

Hints & Tips

_____

_____

_____

_____

_____

_____

_____

_____

_____

_____

_____

_____

_____

Recipe: _____
Serves: _____
Ingredients: _____
_____
_____
_____
_____

Method: _____
_____
_____
_____
_____
_____
_____
_____

Recipe: _____
Serves: _____
Ingredients: _____
_____
_____
_____
_____

Method: _____
_____
_____
_____
_____
_____
_____
_____

Just a Note...
_____
_____
_____
_____
_____
_____

Just a Note...
_____
_____
_____
_____
_____
_____

Hints & Tips

_____

_____

_____

_____

_____

_____

_____

_____

_____

_____

_____

_____

_____

Recipe: _____
Serves: _____
Ingredients: _____
_____
_____
_____
_____

Method: _____
_____
_____
_____
_____
_____
_____
_____
_____

Recipe: _____
Serves: _____
Ingredients: _____
_____
_____
_____
_____

Method: _____
_____
_____
_____
_____
_____
_____

Just a Note...
_____
_____
_____
_____
_____
_____
_____

Just a Note...
_____
_____
_____
_____
_____
_____

Hints & Tips

_____

_____

_____

_____

_____

_____

_____

_____

_____

_____

_____

_____

_____

Recipe: _____
Serves: _____
Ingredients: _____
_____
_____
_____
_____

Method: _____
_____
_____
_____
_____
_____
_____
_____
_____
_____

Recipe: _____
Serves: _____
Ingredients: _____
_____
_____
_____
_____

Method: _____
_____
_____
_____
_____
_____
_____
_____
_____

Just a Note...
_____

_____

_____

_____

_____

Just a Note...
_____

_____

_____

_____

_____

Hints & Tips

Recipe: _____
Serves: _____
Ingredients: _____
_____
_____
_____
_____

Method:
_____ _____
_____
_____
_____
_____
_____
_____

Recipe: _____
Serves: _____
Ingredients: _____
_____
_____
_____
_____

Method:
_____ _____
_____
_____
_____
_____
_____
_____

Just a Note...

_____

_____

_____

_____

_____

Just a Note...

_____

_____

_____

_____

_____

Hints & Tips

Recipe: _____
Serves: _____
Ingredients: _____
_____
_____
_____
_____

Method: _____
_____
_____
_____
_____
_____
_____
_____
_____

Recipe: _____
Serves: _____
Ingredients: _____
_____
_____
_____
_____

Method: _____
_____
_____
_____
_____
_____
_____
_____
_____

Just a Note...

_____
_____
_____
_____
_____

Just a Note...

_____
_____
_____
_____
_____

Chocolate Fudge

MAKES 32 PIECES

INGREDIENTS

- 2 tbsp cocoa powder
- 300 ml/10 fl oz milk
- 125 g/4½ oz plain chocolate, at least 85% cocoa solids, finely chopped
- 800 g/1 lb 12 oz caster sugar
- 125 g/4½ oz butter, chopped, plus extra for greasing
- pinch of salt
- 1½ tsp vanilla extract
- 175 g/6 oz pecan nuts, walnuts or toasted hazelnuts, or a mixture of nuts, chopped

1 Put the cocoa powder into a small bowl, add 2 tablespoons of the milk and stir until blended. Pour the remaining milk into a large, heavy-based saucepan, then add the cocoa mixture and chocolate and simmer over a medium–high heat, stirring, until the chocolate melts. Add the sugar, butter and salt, reduce the heat to low and stir until the butter is melted, the sugar is dissolved and you can't feel any of the grains when you rub a spoon against the side of the pan.

2 Increase the heat and bring the milk to the boil. Cover the pan and boil for 2 minutes, then uncover and carefully clip a sugar thermometer to the side. Continue boiling, without stirring, until the temperature reaches 115°C/247°F, or until a small amount of the mixture forms a soft ball when dropped in cold water.

3 Meanwhile, line a 20-cm/8-inch square cake tin with foil, grease the foil, then set aside.

4 Remove the pan from the heat, stir in the vanilla extract and beat the fudge until it thickens. Stir in the nuts.

5 Pour the fudge mixture into the prepared tin and smooth the surface. Set aside and leave to stand for at least 2 hours to become firm. Lift the fudge out of the tin, then peel off the foil. Cut the fudge into eight 2.5-cm/1-inch strips, then cut each strip into four pieces. Store the fudge for up to one week in an airtight container.

fond memories xx